Out of the Wilderness

Out of the Wilderness

31 Devotions to Walk with God Through
Your Hardest Seasons

ANGELA HALILI AND ARIELLE REITSMA

WaterBrook

WaterBrook

An imprint of the Penguin Random House Christian Publishing Group,
a division of Penguin Random House LLC

1745 Broadway, New York, NY 10019

waterbrookmultnomah.com
penguinrandomhouse.com

Wheat grass art: devastudios/Adobe Stock

Library of Congress Cataloging-in-Publication Data
Names: Halili, Angela, author. | Reitsma, Arielle, author.
Title: Out of the wilderness : 31 devotions to walk with God through your hardest seasons | Angela Halili and Arielle Reitsma.
Description: [Colorado Springs] : WaterBrook, [2025] | Includes bibliographical references.
Identifiers: LCCN 2024056897 | ISBN 9780593602584 (hardcover) | ISBN 9780593602591 (ebook)
Subjects: LCSH: Christian women—Prayers and devotions. | Devotional exercises.
Classification: LCC BV4844 .H255 2025 | DDC 242/.4—dc23/eng/20250123
LC record available at https://lccn.loc.gov/2024056897

Printed in Canada on acid-free paper

2 4 6 8 9 7 5 3 1

FIRST EDITION

The authorized representative in the EU for product safety and compliance is
Penguin Random House Ireland, Morrison Chambers, 32 Nassau Street,
Dublin D02 YH68, Ireland, https://eu-contact.penguin.ie.

BOOK TEAM: Production editor: Laura K. Wright • Managing editor: Julia Wallace •
Production manager: Maggie Hart • Copy editor: Lisa Grimenstein •
Proofreaders: JoLeigh Buchanan and Rose Decaen

Book design by Virginia Norey

For details on special quantity discounts for bulk purchases,
contact specialmarketscms@penguinrandomhouse.com.

To our GGB family, thank you for providing a safe place to share our hearts and our faith. We wouldn't be able to do any of this without you.

And to our Jesus, the light that leads us out of the wilderness. Thank you for saving us. We will never stop telling people what you did for us.

Contents

Out of the Wilderness

Out of the Wilderness

wilderness season: a time of trials, testing, and
spiritual warfare

When you find yourself in a wilderness season, it can feel like you're dying—like you've been abandoned as you cry out for help in your moment of need. But even Jesus spent time in the wilderness, and as Christians we will too.

We may think that by embracing God and our faith, the road will be easier or problem free, but this isn't what we're promised. John 16:33 says, "I have told you these things, so that in me you may have peace. In this world you will have trouble. But take heart! I have overcome the world." We will experience times of hardship, but while the world sees hardship as only that, we need to look at it as an opportunity for growth—an opportunity to put our trust in God and his plans, to surrender ourselves and our lives, knowing that he works all things for good! It's an opportunity to draw closer to him. So when you feel like giving up, when you feel lost or alone, remember that you are not abandoned—you are meant to be right where you are.

We (Ang and Ari) know what it's like to feel lost and broken, unworthy and unqualified, and to feel shame or judgment for our past. We know how hard it is to truly seek God and to surrender the things of this world in order to live a life after Christ. We've personally experienced amazing highs but also some *real* lows, periods where we struggled to hear God's voice and questioned whether he was even listening. In fact, when we first met a few years ago, we were both searching for purpose. I (Ari) woke up on my birthday, feeling utterly alone and heartbroken after my three-and-a-half-year relationship ended, and tried to put on a brave face and make it through the modeling job we were both working that day. During a break, I couldn't help but sob into my hands, unable to compose myself.

That's when I (Ang) saw Ari crying and suddenly felt the Holy Spirit prompt me to approach her. A vulnerability instantly connected us, as we saw our own struggles reflected in the other. In the devotions that follow, you'll read about how our lives were transformed as we came to know Jesus by reading our Bibles together. Up to this point, we were both simply existing, lacking joy and purpose as we fought to gain control over our mental health, our careers, and our relationships, basing our identities on fleeting things that would disappear from our lives and leave us flailing and lost again. We desperately tried to control every area of our lives, thinking that we could determine the outcomes and force our lives to be what we wanted. We looked to the world to find peace but were constantly coming up empty.

But in Jesus, we've found the peace that surpasses all understanding, a peace that exists even in difficult circumstances. We've found a love that never fails, one that always surrounds us. Even when we feel separate or distant from God, we recognize his hand over our lives and hold on to our trust in him, knowing that this trial is only for a season and he will work all things out for our good.

Coming to truly know Jesus through his Word, we found our purpose in starting our podcast, *Girls Gone Bible,* to share our stories and help others find the same peace we've found in him. Our GGB community has become our family, whom we love and pray for daily. Our podcast was the first space we found to share about our love for God and all that he does for us. Despite feeling unqualified to speak about God, we knew he was calling us to step into this space, and after we released the first episode, it became clear how many people were hungry for him. It also showed us how God had been preparing and equipping us to connect with others in this new way. And now we have written the devotional you're holding as a way to share new stories about how God has been working in our lives the past few years to bring us to this point.

This devotional is meant to encourage and strengthen you in your season of struggle and remind you that God is still present and working in your life, even when you can't see or understand his plans. Whether the topic is relationships, careers, friendships, identity, or purpose, or whether you're simply searching for God's voice in the quiet, these devotions include scriptures and truths from our hardest wilderness seasons.

Each day opens with Scripture and a short biblical breakdown of the topic, because we want you to understand the importance of being rooted in God's Word. When we feel like God is silent, or like we can no longer hear him, we need to go to his Word—to the truth. Each day also includes a story from one of us. By learning bits of our stories, you'll see how God showed up when we needed him most and how he used difficult times to challenge and deepen our faith.

We pray that our stories provide hope that God is growing you in your own trials, that he hears you and loves you. In fact, he loves you so much that he allows you to experience the wilderness in the hopes that you fall at his feet.

Your time in the wilderness is only for a season. You have a life of purpose, meaning, and love on the other side, waiting for you to embrace it. We can't promise that by the end of this devotional your wilderness season will have passed, but we hope you will find encouragement, friendship, and godly advice as you journey through it and come out the other side stronger and even more in love with Jesus.

Let's get started, shall we?

Day One

Prepare the Way for the Lord

John replied in the words of Isaiah the prophet, "I am the voice of one calling in the wilderness, 'Make straight the way for the Lord.'"

Now the Pharisees who had been sent questioned him, "Why then do you baptize if you are not the Messiah, nor Elijah, nor the Prophet?"

"I baptize with water," John replied, "but among you stands one you do not know. He is the one who comes after me, the straps of whose sandals I am not worthy to untie."

—John 1:23–27

The one who has the bride is the bridegroom. The friend of the bridegroom, who stands and hears him, rejoices greatly at the bridegroom's voice. Therefore this joy of mine is now complete. He must increase, but I must decrease.

—John 3:29–30, esv

John the Baptist clarified his identity and mission in this passage in John 1. He was not the Messiah, nor Elijah, nor the Prophet. Rather, he was the one preparing the way for the Messiah—Jesus. John's mission was to call people to repentance and baptize them as a symbol of their commitment to change. His role was to ready people to receive Jesus and his message, fulfilling the prophecy of Isaiah and pointing to the greater work that Jesus would accomplish (Isaiah 40:1-9).

In these verses from John 3, John the Baptist expressed his joy and fulfillment in seeing Jesus's ministry flourish. Using the wedding metaphor, he illustrated his supportive role as the friend of the Bridegroom (Jesus), rejoicing in the success and presence of Jesus. John's declaration, "He must increase, but I must decrease," is evidence of his humility and understanding that his purpose was to prepare for Jesus, and now that Jesus had come, John's role would naturally decrease as Jesus's ministry took center stage.

From Angela

Just as John knew his purpose, we, too, possess a deep yearning and essential need to have and know our purpose in life. Chasing empty ideals can leave us feeling unsatisfied, and a lack of purpose will lead to deep depression and a lifetime of emptiness. But as Christians, our purpose is clear: to know Jesus and to make him known. While some may think that sounds cheesy, I know now it is what God wants for me, just like he did for John the Baptist.

While I haven't always walked according to God's Word, I *have* been someone who prays. But honestly, even though I prayed my heart out in my younger days, my prayers were selfish. Back then, I begged God to fulfill my greatest needs and desires. I told him things had to go exactly the way I envisioned or else I'd just die.

But that all changed one day when I was twenty-five and God spoke clearly into my heart and told me that I had my relationship with him backward. He reminded me who was God (*him*) and who was not (*me*). He reminded me that *I* am to serve *him,* not the other way around. I had been treating my relationship with God transactionally, ignoring that he is the giver of life and creator of all, and I am but a servant.

That interaction was one of the greatest moments of maturity in my faith walk. Incredibly humbled, I realized I had a big heart change to make.

Since then, every morning when I wake up, I drop to my knees and ask Jesus what he needs from me. I offer him my day, saying, "I dedicate every moment of today to you. Where do you need me to go? Who do you need me to talk to? How can I serve you in all I do and everywhere I go?" I am now completely Christ-focused, which has changed my life forever. I have the most beautiful relationship with Jesus, in which I know my place as servant and his role as master.

In my submission to God, I found security. And joy. And peace. I discovered purpose like I'd never known before. I soon found a mentor who discipled me and helped me learn more about God and the Bible. But the knowledge I gained wasn't for me alone. It was for me to then go out and make more disciples (Matthew 28:19) by sharing what I learned. I began proclaiming the gospel of Jesus Christ to everyone, telling them what God did for my life and trying my best to articulate that he could do the same for them. I'll explain more about the origins of *Girls Gone Bible* (GGB) in a later devotion, but the seed of its existence was planted in my heart at that time. I want my entire being, my entire existence, to be a means to prepare the way for the coming Lord. Serving God and his people fills my soul to overflowing.

The Bible says the first commandment is to love God, and the second is to love people (Matthew 22:37–39). Although I've always been a lover of people, loving Jesus expanded my heart's capacity for loving others to an extent I didn't even know was possible. Scripture also says that we love because he first loved us (1 John 4:19). This is why loving Jesus is a prerequisite to loving people the way he intends for us to. When I fell in love with Jesus, I could no longer be passive or indifferent about people.

Behind every set of eyes is a soul that Jesus cares about. And since Jesus cares for them, so do I.

In December 2023, Ari and I felt led to host a baptism in L.A. out of this overflowing love of others. Jesus had given us the amazing gift of our GGB community, and it had been growing rapidly. The people in this community became my best friends, whom I get to commune with every Friday through our podcast. They are the ones I spend all week praying for. I care for them so deeply and love them with everything I have. They have loved Ari and me so well, and my life is full because of them.

And though it may have been GGB that drew these people to the L.A. event, it was the one true God, Jesus Christ, whom they came looking for. My heart was forever marked by the brokenness I saw in many who attended, and a burden was placed on my soul that has not lifted and I pray never does. Being able to look into the eyes of so many of our brothers and sisters in Christ—people we had been speaking to through our podcast but hadn't ever met—and to pray for them was a turning point for me. It was a reminder that people are hurting, and they need Jesus.

Yet, even up to this point, I had been attempting to hold on to control of my life. I had my own ideas and plans. That night after the baptism, alone on the couch at 2:00 A.M., I had an intimate moment with God. I whispered, "Jesus, I'm ready to give it all up. Anything I had planned for my life, I'm ready to let it all go for what we did tonight, for the rest of my life." And I meant it.

I constantly pray that God instills in me the heart posture of John the Baptist—that my only aim would be to prepare the way for the Lord's coming, and that the people who hear me and think to follow *me* would immediately recognize the only one worth following is Jesus.

I pray that I will become less and less so that Jesus becomes greater and greater in my place. That when I speak, my words will point to Jesus. That when I move, my actions will point to Jesus. That when I love, my heart will point to Jesus. I am not worthy even to untie his sandal straps, so it is my life's greatest honor to be a small part in the big things only he can do.

Dear God,

Thank you for the gift of your Son, Jesus Christ. Help me to make him known in every aspect of my life. Let my words, actions, and thoughts reflect his love and truth to those around me. Guide me to find my true purpose in Jesus so that I may live a life that glorifies you. Lord, as I seek to be more like Jesus, I also ask for a spirit like John the Baptist's. Give me the courage to speak boldly of your coming kingdom, the humility to always point others to Jesus, and the dedication to prepare the way for him in the hearts of many. Strengthen me to live a life of purpose and service, drawing others to your light. May I decrease so that Jesus may increase in all that I do.

In his name I pray, amen.

Your turn: What have you learned about Jesus in this devotion, and how does this apply to your season in the wilderness?

_____

_____

_____

When Love Left, Jesus Stayed

Just then a woman who had been subject to bleeding for twelve years came up behind him and touched the edge of his cloak. She said to herself, "If I only touch his cloak, I will be healed."

Jesus turned and saw her. "Take heart, daughter," he said, "your faith has healed you." And the woman was healed at that moment.

—Matthew 9:20–22

The Bible's account of the bleeding woman appears amid the larger narrative of Jesus raising a young girl from the dead. The inclusion of the story in three of the Gospels (Matthew, Mark, and Luke) indicates that this miracle is significant. The unnamed woman would've been considered unclean due to her condition, leaving her stigmatized and isolated. By the time she met Jesus, she had heard of his healing ability and was desperate for a cure.

For twelve years, her existence had been one of pain and suffering. But when she brushed Jesus's hem, she was healed. When Jesus asked, "Who touched me?" she came before him.

Where others would have cast her out, Jesus met her with mercy and grace. And while she is unnamed in the Gospels, Jesus named her "daughter" and claimed her as one of his children. Her faith saved her, but it was her pain that drove her toward her Savior. She had tried every cure, but only Jesus could make her whole.

From Arielle

Like the woman who had been bleeding for twelve years, I was also desperate for a miracle. My three-and-a-half-year relationship had ended abruptly in 2022, and it felt like a nightmare I was waiting to wake up from. Anxious, hopeless, brokenhearted, and sleep deprived, I couldn't see the light at the end of the tunnel. I was alive but not living. I was merely trying to survive. The emotional pain was so severe it felt physical, like a sickness with claws so deep it was unbearable. Here I was at thirty, eager to start my life with the person I loved so much and trusted the most—and then suddenly all my dreams of being a wife and mother were gone.

I remember lying on my floor with nothing left in me except my overbearing thoughts. My hands were splayed over my head because I couldn't take another second of the torment and self-blame that were replaying in my mind. *What now? How will I ever recover from this? Where is the person I had trusted? Did I ever even know him?*

After the breakup, I went back to Boston to be with family, but nothing healed the pain. Like the bleeding woman, I tried every physician, but no one could cure me. I lay in my Nan's arms, begging her to take the hurt away. I asked my friends the same repetitive question of what I could have done differently as I wrung my hands in anguish.

"Ari, you've got to eat something. It's been weeks," my dad said. But I couldn't even lift my head off the pillow, let alone eat. So every morning, he put a glass of chocolate milk by my bedside, the only thing I could stomach. I ordered books on depression and heartbreak, which only led me to feel more depressed. The doctors prescribed medications for sleep, but those only made me feel worse when I woke up. In therapy I asked, "Will this ever go away? Will I ever be happy again?"

One night, I mustered up the courage to go out with friends. As everyone was talking and laughing, I noticed I couldn't hear anything they were saying. Everything around me felt like it was caving in. I was in so much physical pain, I thought, *Is it in my head? Am I dying? Why can't I hear anything? Just keep smiling—it's all in my head.*

"Ari, are you okay?"

I stood up . . . and collapsed. Two friends carried me to the car and rushed me to the ER. The pain was so bad I couldn't even see straight. Hunched over, I begged to be admitted to a room. After hours of testing, the doctor told me I had had a nervous breakdown. The emotional pain had taken such a toll on my body that it turned physical. I felt so much shame that I had gotten to this point that I couldn't even tell my family.

I was completely lost and desperate. When I looked in the mirror, I didn't recognize myself. I needed help.

About a week after my trip to the ER, by the grace of God, as I was driving, I noticed a church near my house and pulled in. Inside the empty sanctuary, I fell to my knees, trembling, and cried out, "God, can you help me? I can't do this on my own. I need you. My heart is so broken it feels like I'm not going to make it through."

In that moment, I felt *seen*. I sensed a comfort and a love I had never experienced before, like that of a parent holding me in his arms. I had never known true peace, but in that moment, there it was—the peace I had been searching for my whole life. That was the day I met God.

I became so dependent on him, like a little girl with her dad. I returned to that church frequently, where I would lie in the pews for hours, just being in his presence, talking and crying out to him. It was the only time I felt relief. Because of this newfound peace and love, I longed to be close to him. I started attending church every Sunday, and people would pray for me. But even that wasn't enough to satisfy my hunger for understanding, so I watched sermons at home and learned about who God was.

I believe raw dependency on God comes from deep suffering. He saved my life through my brokenness and showed me true love. Though my healing was not a quick fix, I'm glad it wasn't. My pain had caused me to cling to Jesus's hem, because I had finally found what I longed for. So I held on tight. I told God that I couldn't get through this without him, and I brought every broken piece to him. Soon, my "Why, God?" turned into "Thank you, God."

As I look back on the days I could barely move, the mornings I wished I didn't wake up, the dark nights of pleading and crying and not understanding why the person I had loved most had left, I'm thankful because it led me to the only thing that really matters—God. I couldn't depend on myself or my partner for security, because genuine security is only found in God.

Can you relate? Is your heart so broken you feel like you will do just about anything to heal it? What if in the mastery of God, your broken heart isn't for your disappointment but for your development? Here's what I know: You have a heavenly Father, one who loves you more than anyone else in this entire world ever could. One who wants the very best for you, who will not only bind up your wounds, heal you, redeem you, and never leave you nor forsake you, but who is also a Father who will never withhold something that is truly yours. So when someone or something feels like it has been taken away, it's simply because it is not in God's will. There is something on the other side that he has for you that is so much greater. You just have to trust him with your broken pieces. All it takes is a small seed of faith to bring your sick heart to him.

For as you reach out to him, you, too, can hear his voice gently saying, *Your faith has made you well. Go in peace.*

Dear Jesus,

I pray for my broken heart. You see the brokenness and the pain, you hear the cries of my heart, and as you are building me and healing me, I ask that you give me the strength, comfort, and peace that surpasses all understanding to get me through this. I pray that you will help me to trust in you, to walk by my faith and not by sight. To know that your ways are not my ways, and you are working everything for my good.

I love you. Amen.

Your turn: What have you learned about Jesus in this devotion, and how does this apply to your season in the wilderness?

My Mind Is a War Zone

Though we live in the world, we do not wage war as the world does. The weapons we fight with are not the weapons of the world. On the contrary, they have divine power to demolish strongholds. We demolish arguments and every pretension that sets itself up against the knowledge of God, and we take captive every thought to make it obedient to Christ.

—2 Corinthians 10:3–5

In these verses, the apostle Paul used military terminology to describe how our battle is not against flesh and blood; instead, it's spiritual. And we must fight with God's mighty weapons: prayer, faith, hope, love, God's Word, and the Holy Spirit. God must be the commander in chief, and our thoughts must be under his control if we want a fighting chance in the spiritual battle that is always happening around us. Saying "we demolish arguments and every pretension that sets itself up against the knowledge of God" speaks to the fact that we must tear down every prideful or anti-biblical idea that keeps us from knowing God. Paul then told us to take any thought that is against God or the Word of God—to *capture it*—and yield it to Christ. Otherwise, those thoughts will take us captive. We capture them by immediately recognizing them and bringing them to God in prayer and by speaking God's truth over them.

From Angela

I battled severe anxiety and panic disorder for years before I was diagnosed with OCD. The National Institute of Mental Health describes OCD like this: "Obsessive-compulsive disorder (OCD) is a long-lasting disorder in which a person experiences uncontrollable and recurring thoughts (obsessions), engages in repetitive behaviors (compulsions), or both. People with OCD have time-consuming symptoms that can cause significant distress or interfere with daily life. However, treatment is available to help people manage their symptoms and improve their quality of life."[1]

Even though I was diagnosed with OCD, I reject the idea that it is a part of me or a part of my identity. I do believe I have a genetic predisposition to OCD, and before I was in a true relationship with Jesus, it had a foothold in my life and intensely affected how I lived day-to-day. Today, I keep my OCD under control because of the blood of Jesus that has set me free. When I am weak, vulnerable, or perhaps not in total right standing with God, the enemy—Satan—attacks me with OCD-like thoughts and obsessions.

OCD is something I wouldn't wish on my worst enemy. It makes you feel *craaazyyyy*. And it's so difficult to find the words to accurately describe how it affects your brain. I experienced OCD in the form of obsessive thinking, ruminating thoughts, and repetitive behavior. Most of my OCD centered around fixated thoughts and anxiety that absolutely plagued my life and brain. For example, since I was battling irrational health-related anxiety and always thought something was severely wrong with me, I would feel a sensation in my chest, near my heart, and I would gasp for air, certain I was having a heart attack. This resulted in a perpetual, looping internal battle convincing me of that. *What was that? Was that in my heart? Is something wrong? My heart is in bad condition. I have to see someone. I have to see a doctor. I'm going to have a heart attack, and no one is here to help me. I'm going to end up dead.* I went to the doctor sooo many times, and I did so much blood work and testing, only to be told every single time that my health was in perfect condition. Being told that nothing was wrong while desperately trying to find the answer to what *was* wrong made me feel incredibly hopeless and scared.

Obsessive and irrational fears were a major component of OCD for me. I developed countless fears and phobias: I couldn't go as high as a fourth-floor balcony without experiencing vertigo and getting faint. I had trouble driving for almost three years, and I avoided the highway whenever I could. If I couldn't, I stayed in the very right lane in case I had to urgently pull over due to a panic attack, which was often—like, multiple times every day. I developed agoraphobia, which is the fear of leaving environments you consider to be safe, fearing that you will have a panic attack.

OCD is often linked to addiction issues and disordered eating, both of which I have dealt with. My OCD resulted in an all-or-nothing mentality, which led to an obsessive relationship with alcohol and deeply influenced my relationship with food. It caused me to rely heavily on routine eating and safe foods, and any time that routine was disrupted, all hell would break loose in my mind.

One day in 2022, I was listening to a sermon, and the speaker mentioned 2 Corinthians 10:5, about how we have this ability to take thoughts captive. God spoke to me so clearly through this scripture. For the first time, I understood that I am not a powerless victim to what is going on in my head. I have the ability to take control of these thoughts through the authority given to me by Jesus and the empowerment from the Holy Spirit. At this point, I had already learned the power of speaking Scripture over myself, so every time I would lose control over my thoughts, I would repeat 2 Corinthians 10:5. Over time, my thoughts became obedient to Christ.

Faithful, miracle-working, light-at-the-end-of-the-tunnel Jesus. He didn't leave us as orphans, and he didn't leave us helpless. He left us with tools and practices and promises and the ability to overcome. He saved me. He healed me. I am victorious over OCD because Jesus nailed it to the cross. That doesn't mean it never shows up. But he delivered me. It's up to me to stay delivered by staying close to Christ.

When I was in my early twenties and trying to navigate my declining mental health, I didn't have anyone around me who understood. It hurts to think back to this young version of me, when my own brain was fighting against me. My mind was an absolute war zone. And it hurt. I was in so much emotional pain, with little to no relief. I was also scared—I felt so unsafe in my own head. I now know that Jesus was there, ready to rescue me, waiting for me to reach out to him as my redeemer.

If you are struggling with OCD, anxiety, or any other mental health issue, my heart aches for you. You are not subject to your thoughts. Your thoughts are subject to *Jesus*. You have the mind of Christ, and your mind belongs to him. You are safe. You are protected. Remember, "You keep him in perfect peace whose mind is stayed on you, because he trusts in you" (Isaiah 26:3, ESV).

Dear Jesus,

I thank you that you are Jehovah-Rapha, the God who heals. I declare 2 Corinthians 10:5: "I demolish arguments and every pretension that sets itself up against the knowledge of God, and I take captive every thought to make it obedient to Christ." I have the mind of Christ. Lord, I ask that you release a super-natural healing over my thoughts. I pray that you release a supernatural peace in my mind and that all my thoughts are lovely, pure, and pleasing to you. I pray my mind is set on you. I pray you heal me and deliver me from any hereditary or genetic predisposition to mental health struggles. I trust that you are Lord over my thoughts. I believe that I am safe and healthy. I believe that you are taking care of everything concerning my thought life and mental health. I love you, Jesus. Thank you for keeping me in perfect peace. I fix my eyes on you.

In your name I pray, amen.

Your turn: What have you learned about Jesus in this devotion, and how does this apply to your season in the wilderness?

_____

_____

_____

_____

_____

_____

_____

Day Four

From Lost to Found in His Purpose

What I always feared has happened to me.
What I dreaded has come true.
I have no peace, no quietness.
I have no rest; only trouble comes.
—Job 3:25–26, NLT

Job was a man so righteous and faithful that Satan wanted to test him. Satan believed that if all the good things God had blessed Job with were taken away, Job would turn his back on God. So God allowed Satan to take Job's family, possessions, and health. In the aftermath, Job continually cried out to God. Believing he'd been living a faithful and righteous life, Job begged God for clarification and for mercy. Still, despite everything, Job remained faithful and worshipped God: "Though he slay me, yet will I hope in him" (Job 13:15). In the end, God rewarded and blessed Job again.

Like Job, we cannot see past the present moment, and when things are hard or painful, it's easy to become bitter. But as Christians, our suffering is doing something constructive in us. God will use *everything* for his glory and our good. He can see past the present; he sees the beginning and the end. When things seem the darkest, we should cling most tightly to our faith and put ourselves at the feet of Jesus to seek his mercy and grace.

From Arielle

I'd fought since I was fifteen to build my acting career, which was a huge part of my identity. In fact, it *was* my identity. But being in the entertainment industry was a never-ending uphill battle, where the proverbial door was constantly shut in my face, my appearance and weight were scrutinized, and I rarely got a callback after auditioning. I'd feel elated when I did get a part, then defeated when I'd have to sit for months wishing and hoping to be booked again.

Before Covid-19, I'd had a stable modeling job for six years. But the pandemic basically shut down the industry, including my job. I had made such an idol out of my career that when it was gone, I'd not only lost my job but also my identity. I could not function—I didn't know who I was. As a result, my depression pulled me under, and I couldn't haul myself out. All my job applications were rejected, and my thoughts kept telling me I would never be anything. I couldn't wait for the sun to go down each day because sleep was my only relief, the only time my mind wouldn't race. This industry was all I knew, and, truthfully, because I didn't have a college degree, it was all I thought I *could* do.

At this point, I'd only recently found God. I was early in my journey of discovering who he was, still wary to fully surrender and trust him. Instead, I kept trying to control my life. But because I didn't feel "good enough," I was living in shame. I was sinking, and God seemed so silent. Every day I felt more purposeless.

I realized that trying to control who I was supposed to be and what I was supposed to do was getting me nowhere. I knew I couldn't live and feel like this anymore. So I ran back to the only thing that gave me peace: God. My heart cried out, *God, who have you called me to be?* In that moment, on my hands and knees with tears streaming down my face, I knew what he wanted me to do—surrender. I couldn't place my identity in fleeting things anymore. I had to stop being led by confusion and anxiety; I needed to be led by the Holy Spirit.

Letting go of everything I had known was tough. Though I struggled, I put my pride aside and worked overtime at jobs I didn't want. In that process God showed me that he was right there with me, building me, strengthening me, and teaching me how to become wiser and stronger. He was showing me how to trust him.

Since childhood, I'd really wanted to help people but was never sure how. I'd think, *I'm struggling to help myself, so what do I have to offer others?* During this time of upheaval, God was planting the seeds and opening my heart to the idea that I was capable of more than modeling. Isaiah 60:22 reads, "At the right time, I, the LORD, will make it happen" (NLT).

Soon after this time of growing my relationship with Jesus, I met Angela. I had always wished that I had someone to relate to during my journey, and she became that person for me. We realized that together we could also be that voice for others. We decided to film a video to share our stories about how God had saved our lives.

That became the first episode of *Girls Gone Bible,* and it was the first time I had ever shared my heart so personally and publicly. I was terrified. But afterward, we received a message from someone who watched it: "I was having suicidal thoughts, and your testimony saved my life. I am now chasing God and it's transforming me."

I suddenly realized that *this* was how I was meant to help people. If sharing my struggles and how God saved my life made someone else feel less alone and helped them seek him, then I would spend the rest of my life doing that. All the suffering I'd endured now made sense. God used it for his glory, to lead me to *you.*

I would go through the trials in my life all over again, knowing it brought me to you. If not for the hardship, I would never have been able to relate to or help you. God was working on me, stripping away what wasn't meant for me, to bring me to a purpose that was perfectly aligned with who I am and that glorified and honored him. If I hadn't struggled the way I did, I wouldn't have been so desperate to seek him the way I did.

Maybe you've been waiting so long you wonder if God will ever come through for you. I'm here to tell you that you're right on schedule. You are in God's plan, in his timing. You may feel hidden, but it's because you are hidden in him. In your struggles, he's saying, *Let me mature you. Let me develop you,* because he has purpose for your life. He's doing something so beautiful for you.

Your ultimate purpose is to know God. Then everything else will be added to that. Are you ready to be a testimony for someone else? You have already been a testimony for me and have gotten me through many dark days. Your life has purpose, and every day that you wake up, it's because God has more for you. He has marked you for a purpose. Whatever you're experiencing, there is something that God is trying to build in you and through you to bring you to the next phase of your life. It may not be easy. But it will be worth it.

Father,

I come to you seeking your guidance and wisdom as I yearn for my purpose to align with your perfect will. Help me, Lord, to surrender my own desires. I submit my plans to you, knowing that your plans are greater than my own. I seek your guidance through prayer, meditation on your Word, and listening to your still small voice. May my ambitions be rooted in your love, grace, and truth. Give me the strength to walk in obedience and remain steadfast in times of challenge and opposition, trusting in your provision. Open the doors that align with your will and close the ones that lead me astray. Teach me to find joy in the process of becoming more like you.

Amen.

Your turn: What have you learned about Jesus in this devotion, and how does this apply to your season in the wilderness?

Sobriety Saved Me

Do not get drunk on wine, which leads to debauchery. Instead, be filled with the Spirit.

—Ephesians 5:18

Christians have different opinions about whether drinking alcohol is okay and can even support their views with Scripture. But in this particular passage, Paul specifically called out *drunkenness,* meaning the overconsumption of alcohol, and denounced it. He told believers not to get drunk on wine, which leads to immoral behavior. Instead, he encouraged them to be filled with the Spirit and seek spiritual fulfillment and guidance.

From Angela

Alcohol almost destroyed me. Because of my experience, I have taken a hard stance on overconsuming alcohol or any other substance that alters one's state of mind. I hope my story of how alcohol nearly ruined my life sheds light on the effects of this epidemic.

Since I was a little girl, a looming feeling of danger has haunted me. I've always felt unsafe, and I've always looked to outside sources to feel secure. My brokenness and pain in this area drove me into the arms of a vice that would never actually fulfill me or bring me lasting comfort.

I was only fifteen years old when I realized that I really enjoyed drinking. It's not even that I loved to party; what I loved was the ability alcohol gave me to escape my pain, even at such a young age.

Although alcohol was a part of my life from that early age, it became a real problem in my twenties. It began to dull every part of who God created me to be. It deadened the way I perceived life around me. My childlike wonder for the world and my joyful spirit began to dwindle. All because of alcohol. I should note that my spiritual life was nonexistent during this time.

When I developed an anxiety and panic attack disorder at the age of twenty, I was uneducated and unaware of the psychological and spiritual reality behind what I was experiencing. I was just an incredibly scared girl who was a victim of the war in her own mind. My solution—alcohol—seemed to be the only thing that made me feel better. It eased the anxiety and relieved some of the pain. Escapism became my best friend for the next few years.

Self-medicating with alcohol or any substance is all fun and games until it turns on you. It feels like it's helping, until it's not. This is how the devil works, not just with substance abuse but with any sin in our lives. It's always good in the beginning, shiny and appealing and seductive. But then Satan leads you to your destruction by the very thing that used to feel so good.

Anxiety and alcohol were a deadly duo for me. The more I drank, the worse I began to feel when it wore off. And my tolerance was rising, so I drank more. This is the violently toxic cycle that happens with alcohol. I went from having an unhealthy relationship with alcohol to being totally dependent on it, emotionally and physically. One morning I went to Whole Foods—I hadn't had a drink yet—and within a few minutes of shopping, withdrawal hit and I was shaking uncontrollably. My head was pounding and my ears were ringing as I struggled to remember where I'd parked my car. It was absolutely terrifying to realize that I couldn't even take a short trip to the grocery store without having a drink. The shackles were tight; I was in bondage, and the future did not look promising. At this point, I had everybody close to me praying for me. But I couldn't bring myself to stop, no matter how many times I tried. It hurts my heart to remember how badly I did not want to be doing what I was doing. I just wanted to feel better. I couldn't stand to look at myself in the mirror, and when I did, I didn't recognize the person looking back at me. My eyes were empty and lifeless; there was no joy and no hope in them. I was a dead man walking, and I was really scared.

Have you ever asked yourself, *How did I get here? How could I have let it get this far? How did I allow it to get this bad?* That was where I found myself. I was trapped in an endless cycle: I wanted to numb the underlying pain, so I turned to a vice. The vice produced an immense amount of shame and guilt that I couldn't stand to feel, so I ran back to the vice to drown out the noise. And repeat.

On Thanksgiving 2019, the guy I was dating gave me an ultimatum: If I didn't stop drinking, he wanted nothing to do with me. I believe an accumulation of all those prayers finally made their way to me, and God met me in this moment. A perfect mixture of shame, hopelessness, and self-loathing came to the surface. Complete and total defeat. It's amazing that the moment of what felt like defeat ended up being my moment of absolute victory. I came to the end of myself. I had nothing left to give. And this is where 2 Corinthians 12:9—"My grace is sufficient for you, for my power is made perfect in weakness"—comes to life in my story. I believe I received supernatural deliverance, and God tore down this demonic stronghold that had its claws in me. At the tender age of twenty-three years old, I put down the drink, and I never picked it back up. And I never will for the rest of my life.

I was able to get sober by a supernatural strength and grace that was imparted by God. I stay sober by that same strength and grace that only makes its way to me through the blood of Jesus and finished work of the cross. His grace and strength are what sustain my sobriety, and I've never been arrogant enough to believe it is by my own might. I have a daunting awareness that if I walk away from him, I'll lose it all. It is only by him, from him, and because of him that I am sober and have joy. I owe my entire life to Jesus for the way he saved me.

Sometimes you meet God and you graciously choose to follow him. But sometimes he comes to rescue you. He rescued me out of a disaster I had created. I had crashed through my own life, burning it to the ground, and there wasn't an ounce of me that deserved the grace I received. I should have ended in a much worse position than I did, but his grace covered and protected me when I actively rejected and turned away from him. The intensity of my love for Jesus matches the severity of what he saved me from. I carry a heavy weight of gratitude daily that has forever changed the way I live. I will never be the same after what he did for me. To thank him, I mirror his sacrifice and lay my life down for him like he did for me. I will spend every moment of every day, for the rest of my life, trying to repay him for what he did. I'll never be able to, but I am committed to spending my existence trying. Everything I do, everything I say, everything I am is for the exaltation and exemplification of Jesus Christ.

I've never heard anyone say they regret giving up alcohol. And now I'm asking you to please take an honest look at your relationship with any substance. Does it enhance your spiritual life, add value, and make you more like Jesus? I know—*I know*—you can let go of anything that is not serving you. I have more faith in you than you realize.

Mind-altering substances weaken you and make you vulnerable to spiritual attack. Remember 1 Peter 5:8: "Be alert and of sober mind. Your enemy the devil prowls around like a roaring lion looking for someone to devour."

Dear Jesus,

I thank you for not giving me a spirit of fear, but of power, of love, and of a sound mind. Thank you for your chain-breaking, miracle-working Spirit who has the power to bring me freedom. Who the Son sets free is free indeed, and I pray that you free me from every addiction, bondage, and yoke of slavery that has burdened me. I declare that I am in covenant with the one true God, Jesus Christ. He is my lord and master and the only one I serve. Lord, open my eyes to any addiction, idol, or bad habit in my life, and give me your Holy Spirit to empower me to walk away from it. I receive your freedom and your power.

In your name I pray, amen.

Your turn: What have you learned about Jesus in this devotion, and how does this apply to your season in the wilderness?

Day Six

The Pursuit of Purity

Finally, brothers and sisters, whatever is true, whatever is noble, whatever is right, whatever is pure, whatever is lovely, whatever is admirable—if anything is excellent or praiseworthy—think about such things.

—Philippians 4:8

When God references purity, he's talking about our hearts. It's about the music we listen to, the movies we watch, and the words we speak, as well as how we use our bodies. Though we need to be mindful of all these components of our lives if we want to honor God, the aspect of purity that feels most prominent in our culture, and the one I'll talk about in this devotion, is sexual purity and modesty.

Pursuing purity may seem foreign to you, but doing so is crucial in your walk with Jesus. He wants an intimate relationship with us. He teaches us how to love and honor him so that we can love and honor ourselves and others better. The closer we grow to him, the more we *want* to pursue purity. It's not about shame or guilt; he defeated that on the cross.

From Arielle

At the beginning of my relationship with Jesus, I felt so dedicated to him, as if I were a little girl holding my dad's hand and letting him lead me along despite how scared I was. I surrendered my will to his and began walking away from many things I was doing, wanting to live in a way that would make him proud. I started reading the Bible, which was like entering an exciting new world. Although I wanted to follow every word he said, there was one thing I was still holding on to: sin in romantic relationships. As someone who had formerly lived a worldly life, purity in my dating relationships seemed foreign to me. I always thought sexual intimacy was a part of love with your partner. I didn't understand the idea of waiting for marriage.

Soon after I entered that new season of having God in my life, Angela and I launched the GGB podcast. I also found myself in a new dating relationship at about the same time. All of it was fun and exciting, yet I lacked a sense of peace. I would record the podcast, then come home . . . and my spirit would feel unsettled.

As we discussed the Word of God on the podcast, the topic of sin kept coming up. Our listeners would ask, "Can you please speak on sexual sin and saving yourself for marriage?" Guilt crept up on me. Sin was staring me in the face, and I was pretending it wasn't there. My pride said, *It's no one's business what I do in my relationship. I have been living this way my whole life, so what difference will it make if I change now?*

I felt angry and frustrated. As I kept living the way I wanted, I couldn't understand why I was still feeling broken, confused, and sad. After all, I was reading my Bible and praying every day, living out my purpose of helping others, and enjoying being in a relationship. Yet something was festering inside me. I needed to talk to someone but didn't know who. I didn't have mentors, and I was too embarrassed to open up to anyone at church about my sin, worried I would be shamed because I was in ministry. But there was one person I did have: Jesus. So I asked him for help.

That Sunday, the message from pastor Touré Roberts was "Winning the War Against Temptation." *Really?* I tensed up, my heart beating out of my chest. I wanted to run, but I put my feelings aside and listened. It felt like the pastor was speaking directly to me, talking about how, when he really gave his life to God, he was serious about it. He wanted to walk away from the stuff he was doing, so he surrendered and reduced the amount of sin in his life drastically. But he still held on to one or two things. And as he got closer to the Lord and started leaning more into him, God started highlighting those remaining things in his life, so he tried to let it go—but he was still holding on to that *one* thing. And then he said something that stuck with me: "But the issue is, that one thing was the thing that was keeping me from everything."

He described how he would go to church, hear the Word, and say, "I won't do it again. This is my last time." But then that *thing* would show up again, and he found himself in a sin cycle. He said, "I loved God but I still loved that thing, and it had a hold on me. But there comes a time when that one thing . . . you're going to have to give it up."[2]

Hearing that honesty from a pastor I respected planted the seed for change. Just like him, I was obedient in certain areas, but I wasn't fully walking in the will of God. I would take one step forward, and then two steps back. Until one day I couldn't go back anymore.

Soon after, I had lunch with a Christian friend, and during a random conversation, she said, "We simply can't call ourselves Christians and have one foot in and one foot out." That sentence wrecked me. Slapped with the truth, I didn't know whether to be angry with her or thank her. I went home and cried, and then I later thanked her because she was right. God used her words to speak to me.

Sometimes that's what we need—the cold, hard truth.

God had given me so much grace in my life, but it was no longer an excuse for me to do whatever I wanted. He had saved me and given me life again, yet I was going against his Word. I could not have one foot in and one foot out in my walk with God. I knew if I didn't let go of my selfish desires and serve him fully, God could not take me where he wanted to, just as it says in John 12:26: "Anyone who wants to serve me must follow me. . . . And the Father will honor anyone who serves me" (NLT).

So I ran to God, my prayers turning to tears. I was real and vulnerable as I confessed to my holy Father. And something inside me broke. I went from feeling like I could never overcome my sexual sin to hating the separation it was creating in my life. The anxiety and lack of peace I had felt was from my sin, and now I was laying it at his feet. God delivered me and changed the desires of my heart and replaced them with a deep desire for him.

Although I will always battle temptation—like we all will—I never thought I could live in such fullness the way I do now. I live in holiness daily, with a peace that surpasses all understanding. I am free from bondage, and I live in goodness, faithfulness, and self-control.

Please know that you do not have to be a slave to sin. With God, you are stronger than any thought or temptation the enemy tries to plant in your mind. There is nothing more satisfying to our God than when he sees us laying down the things that don't serve him. When we come to him in a posture of humility, surrendering our desires and resisting temptation, that is when the Spirit begins to lead us to a life of peace and oneness with God. That is when he sets us free: "So if the Son sets you free, you will be free indeed" (John 8:36).

Dear Jesus,

I'm so sorry for all the times I haven't lived in a way that honors you. I repent for my sins and seek your grace in my life. I want to let go of the things that separate me from you. Lord, help me break any strongholds that are keeping me bound in sin. I pray, Jesus, that you help rid me of the desire for things that are not of your heart so that I may abide in you. Keep my heart pure, so I can walk in holiness.

I love you. Amen.

Your turn: What have you learned about Jesus in this devotion, and how does this apply to your season in the wilderness?

Nothing Stronger than My Momma's Prayers

Confess your sins to each other and pray for each other so that you may be healed. The prayer of a righteous person is powerful and effective.

—JAMES 5:16

James encouraged believers to openly admit their wrong-doings to one another. This practice brings about accountability, humility, and support within the Christian community. Following confession, believers are urged to pray for one another, promoting mutual support and intercession.

The healing mentioned in this verse can be understood in both a physical and spiritual sense, depending on the situation. This last part of the verse highlights the effectiveness of prayers from those who live righteously. A righteous person, in this context, is someone who lives in accordance with God's will and maintains a close relationship with him. This sort of prayer is potent and can lead to significant results.

When adversity hits, our first instinct should always be to pray. But the truth is, the times we need to pray the most are often when it's hardest. When we're down and struggling, we need others to lift us up.

When we are too weak to pray, we need other people to lend some of their strength. A burden shared is a burden lightened. We need to humble ourselves to reach out to trusted others for help. It is a gift to share our sins and struggles and receive prayer on our behalf.

From Angela

I've been incredibly blessed to grow up with a mother who loves Jesus. I would describe my mom as being a Spirit-filled Catholic. She grew up in communist Albania where she couldn't be openly religious, so her mom taught her all about Jesus in the secrecy of their home. The first time she was able to enter a church was when she was in her early twenties. She didn't have religion, only relationship, which resulted in her having the purest connection with God I've ever witnessed. My gift of unshakable faith was passed down from her, and hers was passed down from her mom. Throughout my life, I've watched my mom openly and unashamedly cry out to Jesus in times of distress. This is why I worship God the way I do. She is the reason my faith grows even stronger in a storm. She lived out Proverbs 22:6: "Train up a child in the way he should go; even when he is old he will not depart from it" (ESV).

My mom has been a prayer warrior her whole life, and in any situation her first instinct is to pray. When I was a child, she always included me in her prayer time, letting me sit with her and listen while she talked to God. As I got older and began to lose my way, my praying began to dwindle—but hers only got stronger. She stood in the gap, interceding for me when my relationship with God was nowhere to be found due to my rebellious behavior. She covered me in prayer and had my back spiritually. It is by God's grace and Mom's prayers that I stand here today as the woman of God that I am.

When I started dealing with anxiety, my relationship with Jesus wasn't in a place where I felt I could pray for myself. So I would call my mom, and she would pray for me. I had hundreds of panic attacks over the span of four years, and each time that I called my mom in Florida from Los Angeles, she would pray through them with me. I didn't even have words to explain what I was feeling when she answered the phone. I would simply say, "Mom, I'm not feeling good." And she would know exactly what I meant and begin to pray. We would recite the Lord's Prayer together, over and over, until I calmed down. I get emotional thinking of what I put her through during that time. I know she wouldn't have wanted it any other way, but I'm sure it's crushing for a mother to know her child, especially so far away, is suffering so deeply and is so scared.

I remember when I had one of the most intense panic attacks ever as I was driving over a bridge in L.A. My entire body went numb, and I felt like I almost lost my vision completely. Doom and fear overtook my whole body, and I was certain this was going to be the one that took me out. I had to pull over before I'd even exited the bridge. The panic was so extreme I actually got out of my car . . . on the highway . . . on a bridge. Incredibly dangerous. But I had lost it at that point. I did the only thing I knew to do—I called my mom. And it saddens me to think of what my phone call did to her. She answered the phone to her only daughter screaming and crying, telling her that something was really wrong. "I'm not okay. I am not okay. I want to be normal. I can't take this anymore! I don't want to live anymore if I have to live like this!"

My mother did the only thing *she* knew to do—she cried with me. And she screamed out to Jesus, declaring that I was safe and protected in his name. She calmed me down enough to get me back into the car. Then she had me close my eyes and imagine Jesus sitting in the seat next to me. She told me to keep my eyes closed until I finally saw the face of Jesus and nothing else. She was so strong and calm for me, all while agonizing internally. I'm so sorry for what she had to go through, but I'm so grateful to have such a warrior praying with me and for me when I am too broken to pray for myself.

Reaching out to friends and family in times of need is what my life was built on. These days, first and foremost, my help comes from the Lord. Now that I have reestablished my relationship with God, I am adamant about turning to him for help before going to others. However, God does encourage us to lean on community when we need it. Proverbs 17:17 says, "A friend loves at all times, and a brother is born for a time of adversity." While the temptation is to isolate, we must force ourselves to reach out to people we trust when we are not well, when we are struggling, when we have fallen into sin, and when we can't see God clearly. I implore you, my friend, to confess to someone when something is wrong, to be honest about where you are, and to ask for help.

Dear God,

I thank you for being a good father who cares for my problems. Lord, I ask that you give me a heart of humility, that I may be so humble as to admit my weaknesses and confess my sins. I pray, God, that you would introduce me to godly community that I can lean on for help. I pray that you create in me a heart that is open to receiving support. I pray against all pride or ego that might stop me from being honest about what is actually going on in my life. I receive and am expectant of the godly community you have for me. Send others to stand in the gap for me and give me opportunities to do the same for them. You provide all things, and I thank you for it. I love you so much.

In Jesus's name I pray, amen.

Your turn: What have you learned about Jesus in this devotion, and how does this apply to your season in the wilderness?

Day Eight

Battling Insecurity

Moses said to the LORD, "Oh, my Lord, I am not eloquent, either in the past or since you have spoken to your servant, but I am slow of speech and of tongue." Then the LORD said to him, "Who has made man's mouth? Who makes him mute, or deaf, or seeing, or blind? Is it not I, the LORD? Now therefore go, and I will be with [you]."

—EXODUS 4:10–12, ESV

We all deal with insecurity. We feel inadequate, unprepared, or just downright unqualified. We listen to lies the enemy feeds us that tell us we aren't good or capable enough, that nothing we do makes a difference. The longer we listen to those lies without replacing them with the truth, the more our insecurities grow, holding us back from the person we're called to be. How do we battle insecurity? By remembering who God says we are in his Word.

When chosen to bring God's people out of Egypt, Moses resisted. He had a speech problem that made him feel unqualified, but God reminded him that our strength and our abilities don't come from ourselves—they come from God. Our weakest moments are when God's strength shines.

The enemy knows that if he can keep us focused on ourselves and our faults, he can hide our true identities and destroy what God intended for us to be. In fact, God will often put us in situations where we feel unqualified, because he chooses people with willing hearts and then equips them for the tasks. You see, God chooses those in whom he can develop a strong root system. It's to his advantage to choose those who don't feel qualified for the job because they are less likely to think they can rely on themselves. Faith is established by trust, not understanding. When God asks us to step out in faith, it often makes no logical sense to us. We won't feel qualified, gifted, or educated enough, but that's a great place to be because God is more than enough.

You were never meant to be the best, the brightest, the sharpest, or anything other than who you are. When God called you, he knew what he was getting. It is never about who you are; it's about who he is. Trust his strength, not your limitations, and he will work through you.

From Arielle

One of my biggest weaknesses is my sense of self-worth. I've always struggled with it, specifically when it comes to learning. It takes me a lot longer than the average person to learn things, which has always made me insecure. I remember panicking in school when the teacher would ask me a question on the spot, because it took me longer to process and understand. I dreaded it. I wanted so badly to be like the other kids and learn quickly and do well in school. Some kids wouldn't even study and yet get straight A's, while I would study for hours and still struggle.

My insecurity followed me when Angela and I started GGB. I had only recently started reading the Bible, so I felt inadequate, thinking, *Who am I to speak about God?* I didn't know all the stories or scriptures. How was I going to speak on camera when my low self-confidence made it difficult to even look people in the eye? I had been struggling with my mental health and could barely form sentences. I was so nervous. I didn't feel qualified, and it took me back to that same feeling of insecurity I had in high school.

The first time we went into the studio to film, I looked at Angela and said, "I can't do this. I'm just not good enough for this. I'm stuttering, and no one is going to care what I have to say. I really think you need to find someone more qualified for this." I knew how God was saving my life and how he was healing my mental health, but I wasn't familiar enough with theology to have any sense of confidence.

Angela looked at me and said, "Oh yes, you are. There's no one else I would want to do this with. All you have to do is speak from your heart and let God lead."

Later that day I went home and got down on my hands and knees, going back and forth in conversation with God. "God, I just don't think I can do this. What will people think? How will I get on camera and preach your name when I'm just learning the Bible? I know I can't read the Bible quickly; it takes me a while to really understand and learn. I also worry that my struggles and everything that I have been through are far too embarrassing for me to talk about. What will people think?"

As I sat silently with God, my eyes closed, I had flashbacks of the moments of suffering I had experienced that year. Then I saw a vision of myself in a long white dress, and I was in God's right arm as he was raising me up, healing me. I looked strong, healed, and confident. When I opened my eyes, I had an overwhelming sense of peace. I opened my Bible app, and the verse of the day was Isaiah 41:10:

> So do not fear, for I am with you;
>   do not be dismayed, for I am your God.
> I will strengthen you and help you;
>   I will uphold you with my righteous right hand.

I couldn't believe it. That scripture was so close to the vision I had just had! In that moment, I couldn't even explain it; all I could do was cry tears of joy. God was speaking right to me.

When I read in Exodus 4 about Moses and his struggle with self-worth, I felt the presence of God all around me. I was just like Moses, feeling inadequate to serve the Lord. But God said to him, "I will be with you," and I can't even begin to explain how comforting that felt. God was speaking to me through his Word.

The next day, when we went to record the podcast, I remembered what God told Moses: *I am with you.*

After we released the first GGB video, people from all over sent messages—thanking us, telling us how God had used us to speak to them, and sharing how much it helped them. I realized that through my pain I was helping others. How can I now, for even a second, worry about what people will think or that I will say the wrong thing? It's not about *my* life, because my life is not my own. When I accepted Christ as my Savior, the Holy Spirit came to reside in me so that I am now a temple of God. It isn't about me. It's *all* about Jesus.

You may feel disqualified like I did, having feelings of shame and unworthiness. But please understand that all shame comes from Satan. He says that you're never going to get it right, that you're not good enough. Those lies hide your true identity. And he knows that if he can hide that, he can destroy what God intended you to be. We can only know ourselves through Jesus.

Why don't we feel confident or capable? Because we play the old tapes, listening to what our parents said, what our teachers or our enemies or the media said. But what does God say about you? He says that you are accepted, you are loved, and you are capable.

So how do you get unstuck in your mind? You start believing what God says about you in the Bible. You keep affirming what he says. Take the Word of God and start memorizing it. Psalm 18:32; Jeremiah 29:11; Psalm 139:14; and 2 Timothy 1:7 are great places to start. And when the enemy tries to creep in with negative thoughts or thoughts that don't belong to God, recite 2 Corinthians 10:5 out loud: "I demolish arguments and every pretension that sets itself up against the knowledge of God, and I take captive every thought to make it obedient to Christ." You can change what you allow in your mind and take hold of your true identity.

Dear God,

Help me to see myself the way you see me. When I doubt myself, fill me with your love, truth, and strength. Remind me that I am your child and you are with me. Give me the courage to release my insecurities and answer when you call me, and remind me that these things aren't through my strength but through yours. In my weakness, your strength is made perfect. I love you.

In Jesus's name, amen.

Your turn: What have you learned about Jesus in this devotion, and how does this apply to your season in the wilderness?

_____

_____

_____

_____

The Pure in Heart Will See God

Blessed are the pure in heart,
for they will see God.
—Matthew 5:8

Flee from sexual immorality. All other sins a person commits are outside the body, but whoever sins sexually, sins against their own body. Do you not know that your bodies are temples of the Holy Spirit, who is in you, whom you have received from God? You are not your own; you were bought at a price. Therefore honor God with your bodies.

—1 Corinthians 6:18–20

"The pure in heart will see God" is a phrase from the Beatitudes, a part of Jesus's Sermon on the Mount in the New Testament of the Bible. This verse highlights the idea that those who maintain purity and sincerity in their intentions and actions will have the ability to perceive and understand God's presence more deeply. This purity is often interpreted as a spiritual and moral quality that aligns one with God.

First Corinthians 6:18–20 emphasizes the importance of sexual purity for Christians, rooted in the understanding that their bodies are sacred temples of the Holy Spirit. By avoiding sexual immorality, believers honor God, acknowledging the profound significance of Christ's redemptive sacrifice and his divine presence within them.

From Angela

Purity, in biblical language, is to be morally clean, without blemish. When I was painfully lukewarm and of the world, the concept of Christian purity was always something I looked at with judgment. I also thought purity pertained only to the idea of abstaining from sex outside of marriage; however, abstinence is only a small portion of what purity entails.

The world is constantly indoctrinating us through society and mainstream media. Women are taught at a very young age that sex sells. We wrap our identities in being beautiful, sexy, flirty, and fun, hoping that when men find us attractive, it will fill the God-sized void in our hearts. I grew up trying to present myself in a way that was appealing to men because that was all I knew. I loved Jesus, but I didn't grow up in a culture where pursuing and maintaining purity was even a thought. I did not know that being provocative and immoral was contributing to evil, or that the amount of skin I was showing and my demeanor of immodesty was causing my brothers to stumble.

But my gracious and merciful God began to reveal that this area of my life was my greatest weakness. He led me to understand that the impure relationship I was in was killing me spiritually. He began to deconstruct my whole concept of purity and modesty, and I felt the pressure. The wages of sin are death, and I came to believe that this sin was leading me to my destruction. It was death to my joy, to my peace, to my spiritual life, and death to my ability to hear God's voice. My heart was not pure, and it affected my ability to enter God's presence or walk in accordance with his will.

But this sin was such a part of my life. To give it up frightened me to my core because I did not know love without it. Frankly, I didn't know *myself* without it. It was a key part of who I was, and I was afraid of having to live without it.

But God. He loves us so much he forces us to face the things we would rather pretend aren't there. He tore down the lies I spent my whole life believing. He brought beautiful Christian women into my life, women whose purity and modesty were evident, and held up a mirror to show me things about myself I certainly did not want to see. He made me see them because he loves me too much to let me be anything less than the woman he's called me to be.

During this time, I encountered women who actually honored God with their bodies, and it made me sick thinking about how I'd fallen so short. As this became a conversation in my life, I remember one day returning home and being wrecked with conviction, godly sorrow, and a good amount of shame. I looked at myself in the mirror and played in my mind a cinematic recap of all the mistakes I'd made throughout my life. The memories got louder, and I began to shrink into myself. And then God met me in that bathroom, and he gave me a vision. I saw myself as a little girl in my childhood home. This small version of me was so incredibly innocent and free; she had yet to be tainted by the world or take on identities that were never meant to be hers. And I heard God gently tell me, *You can have this innocence back.* I fell to my knees and cried out to him in full surrender and full understanding of how to move forward.

God is in the business of restoration. Anything that has been taken from you, he can and will restore. The beautiful thing about purity is that it's not something that's lost; it's something that's pursued. I realized I could decide, in that moment, that regardless of what had happened in the past or how I'd lived my life, I could honor God in everything I did from that point forward. By the grace of God and the power of the Holy Spirit, I laid down the sin that according to 1 Corinthians is the only sin committed against your own body. Something I thought I could never live without has been the easiest and most rewarding thing to remove from my life. Praise God.

Biblical purity encompasses a complete sense of moral integrity and righteousness that extends far beyond sexual morality. Biblical purity is very much related to the heart, calling attention to the importance of inner moral and spiritual integrity. Jesus emphasizes that everything we do must stem from pure motives, that purity is not just about having clean hands (external actions) but a pure heart and thought life.

The Holy Spirit has done a beautiful and gentle work in my heart when it comes to modesty. He completely changed the desires of my heart. I don't want to present myself the way I used to. He spoke truth into me and gave me the revelation of who I am in Christ. I understand what it means to be a woman of God and no longer need validation from men, because the love of the Father is what fulfills me. I don't want to be considered sexy; I want to be respected and seen as a powerful ambassador for Christ. In this way, I not only honor God, but also my future husband by keeping myself pure, holy, and blameless in the sight of the Lord. I think about my future husband often, and someday, when we are in covenant, he will have me—mind, body, and spirit. And I delight in the fact that until then, and after then, I belong to Jesus—mind, body, and spirit.

Dear God,

I come before you with a humble heart, seeking your grace and strength. Lord, I desire to live a life that honors you in every way. I pray that you keep me pure, both physically and emotionally. Guard my heart and mind, and help me to abstain from any impure behavior or thoughts that do not align with your will. I declare today that I leave behind any and all sexual immorality and I consecrate myself to the Lord, to be his fully, mind, body, and spirit.

Father, cleanse my heart of any pride, envy, or malice. Fill me with your Holy Spirit, that my intentions may be pure, my actions righteous, and my thoughts centered on your truth. Help me to love others genuinely, to act with humility, and to seek your righteousness in all I do. Thank you for your unwavering love and mercy. May my life be a testimony to your grace, and may I grow each day in holiness and purity, drawing closer to you.

In Jesus's name, I pray. Amen.

Your turn: What have you learned about Jesus in this devotion, and how does this apply to your season in the wilderness?

The Power of the Tongue

Let no corrupting talk come out of your mouths, but only such as is good for building up, as fits the occasion, that it may give grace to those who hear.
—Ephesians 4:29, esv

If anyone speaks, they should do so as one who speaks the very words of God. If anyone serves, they should do so with the strength God provides, so that in all things God may be praised through Jesus Christ. To him be the glory and the power for ever and ever. Amen.
—1 Peter 4:11

From the fruit of their mouth a person's stomach
    is filled;
    with the harvest of their lips they are satisfied.
The tongue has the power of life and death,
    and those who love it will eat its fruit.
He who finds a wife finds what is good
    and receives favor from the Lord.
—Proverbs 18:20–22

Our words have power. Maybe we hear that all the time, but too often we're careless with our words, whether it's cursing, gossip, or speaking negatively about ourselves and others. Our words hold the power of life and death and are what bear fruit. Love, joy, peace, patience, kindness, goodness, faithfulness, gentleness, and self-control should come from the words we speak. When we follow Jesus's example and walk like him, this fruit will be produced in our lives, and we'll see the difference. But if our words are something we're struggling with, we need to take it before God. We must ask the Holy Spirit to guard our tongues, to help us speak blessings instead of curses. He cares about us and wants us to bring our problems to him, so he can help. He gives us feelings of conviction not so that we wallow in guilt, but so that we can seek him and begin to change.

From Arielle

I grew up in Massachusetts, in a place where cussing was like a native language. It seemed foreign to me *not* to swear. That's just how we spoke in our household, day to day. To be honest, I didn't see it as a bad thing. There was something incredibly satisfying about using the strongest word possible to communicate emotion. Our only rule was to never speak that way in front of elders or teachers.

Then in L.A., as I was growing in my faith, I learned what was right and what was wrong. What made it more challenging was that I didn't have mentors. I didn't have Christian community. It was only by the transformative work of the Holy Spirit that I was changing.

One day, I was watching a sermon on conviction. The pastor said, "Some Christians like to say, 'My God doesn't mind if I swear.'" He went on, "Well, what God do you serve? That's not the Jesus that sits at the right hand of God." He continued, "Let's put it this way—would you use cuss words if you were sitting with Jesus? If your answer is no, then why would you continue to speak like that in everyday life?"

I immediately felt convicted. *No,* I thought, *I would never speak that way in front of Jesus, and if I have the Holy Spirit dwelling inside of me, why am I speaking this way?* That was the moment the Holy Spirit spoke to me.

My story with swearing makes me think of the movie *Liar Liar* with Jim Carrey, where a little boy makes a wish that his dad would stop lying, and the wish comes true. The next day, lies cannot come out of his dad's mouth, all because of the wish the boy made. In my case, I was convicted by the pastor's words, so I asked the Holy Spirit to help me with my mouth. From that point on, it was as if swear words could not come out of my mouth.

Some people may think there's nothing wrong with cussing. In my mind, however, you cannot live in holiness while also using foul language; sacred words and filthy words should not come from the same mouth. In my case, quitting swearing—a small act of sacrifice—made me a better person. Without that language, I was more peaceful. If the Holy Spirit is living within us, the natural outpouring of our behaviors will be love, joy, peace, patience, kindness, goodness, faithfulness, gentleness, and self-control (Galatians 5:22–23). Using foul language is the exact opposite of those things.

If you're still questioning whether cussing is right or wrong, ask the Holy Spirit. When you truly have him dwelling inside of you, he will convict you if it's wrong. You won't need outside opinions. And if you're thinking, *This is too hard for me,* know that this is coming from a girl who never imagined she could or would stop swearing.

Dear Jesus,

I love you, Lord. I pray that you would help me to walk and speak more like you every day. Help me to speak only blessings and to use my mouth in a way that honors you. I ask that you remove any unclean words from my tongue and keep only the things that share your joy, your peace, your kindness, your faithfulness, your goodness. I am weak, and only in your strength am I able to overcome. I love you and thank you for the blessings you've placed in my life. I pray you remind me to speak with kindness and a grateful heart.

In your name, amen.

Your turn: What have you learned about Jesus in this devotion, and how does this apply to your season in the wilderness?

_____

_____

_____

_____

_____

_____

_____

_____

_____

_____

Day Eleven

Becoming a Girl Gone Bible

In the beginning was the Word, and the Word was with God, and
the Word was God. He was with God in the beginning.
—JOHN 1:1–2

In this passage, the apostle John revealed the deity of Jesus
and identified him as the preexistent Word, who is both God and with
God. The phrase "in the beginning" echoes the opening of Genesis 1:1,
signifying that "the Word" existed before creation, thus indicating an
eternal presence.

In Hebrew scripture, "the Word" was an agent of creation and another expression for God. John was indicating an intimate relationship
between the Word and God, signifying that the Word is not a separate
god but shares the same essence and being as God. John introduced the
concept of the Trinity, where the Word (later identified as Jesus Christ)
is fully divine and one with God the Father. "He was with God in the
beginning" signifies that Jesus Christ was alive long before his earthly
birth in a manger. He is as present in the Old Testament as he is in the
New.

From Angela

I'll never forget the day I walked into Mosaic Church in Hollywood for the first time. Prior to that, I had never stepped foot in a non-Catholic church. I had never opened a Bible. I wouldn't have been able to recite even one piece of Scripture to you. I knew the basic gospel, loved Jesus with my whole heart, and was encountering the Holy Spirit daily, but I was still missing one absolutely vital part of my faith—the living and active Word of God.

I remember experiencing total culture shock walking into this church building—the worship music, the lights, everybody with their hands lifted high and singing the words on the screen. Having grown up as a conservative Catholic, I was confused by what I saw. But I worshipped with everyone else and sat down when it was time for the Word. The scripture from John 1:1–2 appeared on the screen, words I had never seen before. I instantly felt my spirit light up, which confused me because I didn't understand why this elicited such a reaction in me. How could words I'd never read before feel so familiar? Somehow, I knew these weren't just words. There was incredible weight to them, and I needed to explore what was happening.

I went home and immediately opened my Bible for the first time in my life. And in an instant, I was changed forever. I began in the book of John, and again, those first verses instantly revealed to me the nature of the Holy Trinity and the reality of Jesus as not just my savior, but my creator as well. I didn't make it through the first chapter before breaking down in tears. The presence of God filled my bedroom and wrapped around me like a warm hug as I realized the words were a love letter from my Jesus himself. The Bible was coming to life before my very eyes, and he was speaking to me with every single verse. As Hebrews 4:12 says,

"For the word of God is living and active, sharper than any two-edged sword, piercing to the division of soul and of spirit" (ESV).

I was crying for two reasons: First, I realized that God had written me a love letter and I would never have to guess what he had to say or what he thought about any given situation. Everything he could ever say to me was written in those pages. He left us with a book that provides us with everything we would ever need here on earth. He cares about us so much and wants us to know him so deeply and intimately that he gave us the greatest resource of all time. Second, I was crying because I felt sad that I'd had God's living Word sitting next to my bed my entire life and I never once picked it up. My sorrow was for all I had missed out on.

After that experience, I developed an unquenchable thirst and hunger for God's Word. You could say that's when I became a Girl Gone Bible. I simply fell in love. Every time I opened the Bible, I immediately entered his presence. I realized that these words *are* him. Every verse, every passage, every page brought me deeper and closer to him. I fell in love with learning about him and his life, the beginning of creation, and the history of my faith. I would leave in the middle of hangouts with friends because I missed him and wanted to get back in the Bible. It's as if I was making up for lost time. To this day, I am still in love with and in awe of the Scriptures. It's one of my favorite parts about being a Christian.

As I started reading the Bible, I realized that one of the contributing factors to my being a lukewarm Christian my whole life—and being someone who didn't abide by anything that Jesus would want from me—was that I didn't know him. I *thought* I knew him, but I don't believe anyone can know or even really love Jesus correctly without reading the Bible. How can you love someone you don't know? It was through reading the truth about God and his creation that I fell *in love* with him. And more than that, I developed a healthy, holy, reverent, *intense* fear of the Lord. The revelation of who God created me to be, and the standard I should live my life by according to the Bible, radically changed my life. I realized that God is holy, and I am made in his image, so my aim should be to pursue holiness. First Peter 1:15–16 tells us: "But just as he who called you is holy, so be holy in all you do; for it is written: 'Be holy, because I am holy.'"

I hold the Scriptures in such high esteem because it brought order and structure to my life. It is my guidebook and source of direction. I lean into Psalm 119:105: "Your word is a lamp to my feet and a light to my path" (ESV). God's Word is the number one way I hear from God. Other people may beg him for dreams, visions, and a supernatural word, but whenever someone tells me they're struggling to hear from God, I reply, "Hey, there's this book, and it has everything he would ever say to you in it!"

I hold tight to 2 Timothy 3:16–17, which says, "All Scripture is breathed out by God and profitable for teaching, for reproof, for correction, and for training in righteousness, that the man of God may be complete, equipped for every good work" (ESV). Being educated by the Holy Spirit through his Word is the greatest and most precious education we could receive—more valuable than any college degree.

We live in a world where the truth and lies are always battling for our attention and belief. The Holy Spirit is the Spirit of Truth, and the devil is the father of lies. God invites us to worship him in Spirit and in truth, while the devil speaks and tries to convince us of lies all day long. The greatest way to combat these lies is to know the *truth* of God's Word. Read it, know it, live it.

The Word of God is my anchor and lifeline. It is my only steady and reliable possession here on earth, the only place I can faithfully put my trust. While you and I can change our minds every hour, and our world and culture shift constantly, the Word of God is the same yesterday, today, and forevermore. All things are fleeting, but the Word of the Lord is eternal: "Heaven and earth will pass away, but my words will never pass away" (Matthew 24:35).

Dear God,

Thank you for your precious Word that is more valuable to me than gold. Develop in me, Lord, a heart that is hungry for your Word. Make me feel dependent on your Word, that I would wake up daily and recognize my need for it. That I will not live on bread alone but on every word that proceeds from your mouth. I pray, God, that I would not look at reading the Bible as a chore or part of a checklist, but that I would read it to know you better. I pray that you give me understanding and interpretation of the Scriptures. Open my heart, Lord, and reveal to me the truth behind the words I read. Speak to me through Scripture and give me ears to hear you. I love you. Thank you for your Word.

In Jesus's name, amen.

Your turn: What have you learned about Jesus in this devotion, and how does this apply to your season in the wilderness?

Day Twelve

God's Comfort in Loneliness and Loss

We know that all creation has been groaning as in the pains of childbirth right up to the present time. And we believers also groan, even though we have the Holy Spirit within us as a foretaste of future glory, for we long for our bodies to be released from sin and suffering. We, too, wait with eager hope for the day when God will give us our full rights as his adopted children, including the new bodies he has promised us. We were given this hope when we were saved.

—ROMANS 8:22–24, NLT

When Adam and Eve were tricked by Satan, death, sin, and decay entered the world. In contrast, Romans 8 brings hope and reminds us of our true home, the one our souls ache for.

Our hearts yearn to be with God, and nothing else on earth can satisfy that longing. God knows us; he knows our struggles, hopes, and dreams. He knows what we need.

When I (Ari) was really struggling, God brought me a companion—a dog named Riley—who filled a hole in my heart. While I struggled to hear God's voice and felt abandoned during this time, I now look back and see his fingerprints on every moment. The companionship was only temporary, but it gave me strength and love at a time when I desperately needed it.

Saying goodbye to anything is hard, but death and loss are a natural part of our lives here on earth. God provides comfort in our losses and uses our pain to bring us closer to him. This world is just temporary—our true life, our true reward, is on the other side of eternity.

From Arielle

At eighteen, I moved from Boston to L.A., the boldest and most frightening thing I'd ever done. Moving to a place where I knew no one made me lonesome.

My hole-in-the-wall apartment in Hollywood was the first place I'd ever lived on my own, and I didn't have a lot of money. Home was a six-hour plane ride away, and I had no idea what to do with myself every day with no job and no friends. After job interviews each day, I'd spend hours aimlessly walking through Target because I had nothing else to do.

After about nine months, I had picked up a few modeling jobs, and a new coworker invited me to a barbecue. That's where I met Riley. I had never experienced a connection the way I did with Ry on this God-ordained day. With big brown eyes, a little wiggle bum, and a button nose, this sweet eight-pound shih tzu/Yorkie mix begged me to pick him up. He lay in my arms like a baby, not wanting me to let him down. I'd never felt such an enormous amount of love so quickly. It must have been mutual, because his owner—my coworker—said, "I've never seen him like this with anyone." When it was time to go, I didn't want to leave him, but he wasn't mine.

In the following days, all I could think about was Ry. Although I'd never had a dog growing up, many of my friends did. I remember watching the incredible bond between them and their dogs, and I had always wanted that for myself.

A week later, my coworker called me. He said that Riley hadn't stopped crying since I'd left the night of the barbecue. He also told me that he was having health issues because he was allergic to the dog. He asked if I wanted to adopt him. Of course I did! That day changed my life. He became my boy. My best friend. My angel. We did everything together. He was the absolute joy of my life.

God knew exactly what I needed. Riley gave me purpose, taught me unconditional love, and helped calm my anxiety. Nights alone didn't feel so lonely anymore, and he soothed all my hard moments. The mornings I would wake up with Ry on my chest, staring with his big button eyes as he patiently waited for me to get up, were the best days. His walks were his happy times. Because I struggled with anxiety, it was hard for me to get out and do things, but Ry gave me the push to be active. Having him as a companion helped me to be bolder and try new things. I loved his perseverance and desire to be included, always right by my side in everything. It's funny now how I would get annoyed when people called him a dog because he was "my boy."

And then one morning something looked different. His lip was swollen, so I took him to get checked. They said it was nothing, just a benign lump, and they would remove it. *Phew. Thank you, God.* But two weeks before Riley's surgery, I took him with me to Boston. There I noticed the lump was bigger, so I took him to a second vet. When the phone finally rang with news, it wasn't good. Riley had been misdiagnosed. "Arielle, I'm sorry, but your boy has cancer. He has about four months left."

Cancer? Four months?

The world stopped. You know those moments when your whole nervous system goes into a complete state of shock, when you go completely numb and are in denial? That was me. *He has to be fine.* "What can we do?" I finally asked.

The doctor said, "Well, with chemo, he has about a 20 percent chance of having it go into remission. But it's not cheap."

When the shock wore off, reality hit me like a ton of bricks. *My boy has cancer.* This was the middle of the Covid-19 pandemic, and I was unsure when I'd even work again. But I would've done anything to save Ry, as long as he was not in any pain and could enjoy life. I was committed to trying to save him and to keep him as happy as possible. After the first week of treatments, things seemed to be going well. But by the next week, the cancer had spread. This went on for about nine months. The emotional toll was indescribable. Although it was gut-wrenching, I never took one walk, beach day, or second for granted during those next nine months.

On July 3, 2021, I knew I had to put my boy down. Even as I write this, I still have that same lump in my throat that I did when I lost him. I'll never forget taking one last walk together, and with nothing left in him, we lay in the field—him with his head on my chest, just like the first day I met him. My grief journey was hard. Coming home to an empty house without Riley waiting excitedly by the door was heartbreaking, but waking up was the hardest. Some days I woke up thinking he was there before remembering he was gone.

That's one reason Romans 8 now brings me so much comfort. Although I don't have my best friend physically with me, I close my eyes and picture him running the endless fields, cancer-free, under the golden sun in heaven, till we see each other again.

What a gift from God that we can experience pure love like that! I look back on those moments when I felt God was absent and realize his hand was all over the situation. I had been lonely and sad, and God brought Ry to me as a comfort when I needed it most. Some of my greatest moments were in those last nine months with Ry, and the reasons why God sent him to me all made sense in the last minutes of putting Riley to sleep. I had such peace seeing him in the light of God with no more suffering. And Jesus reminded me of what he says in Luke 23:43, "Truly, I say to you, today you will be with me in paradise" (ESV).

Dear Jesus,

Thank you for always being with me. I pray that in my grief you comfort me with your love and strength. I can't do this without you, Jesus, because the grief is too painful. I pray for peace, that you would send an army of angels to surround me and hold me up in my weakness and help me through my dark days. Lord, I cry out to you to bind up the broken parts of me that need healing.

Jesus, I love you. Amen.

Your turn: What have you learned about Jesus in this devotion, and how does this apply to your season in the wilderness?

We Who Wrestle with God

Jacob was left alone, and a man wrestled with him till daybreak. When the man saw that he could not overpower him, he touched the socket of Jacob's hip so that his hip was wrenched as he wrestled with the man. Then the man said, "Let me go, for it is daybreak."

But Jacob replied, "I will not let you go unless you bless me."

The man asked him, "What is your name?"

"Jacob," he answered.

Then the man said, "Your name will no longer be Jacob, but Israel, because you have struggled with God and with humans and have overcome." . . .

The sun rose above him as he passed Peniel, and he was limping because of his hip.

—Genesis 32:24–28, 31

Jacob wrestled with God in a moment of intense personal crisis and transformation. Leading up to the encounter, Jacob was preparing to meet his estranged brother, Esau, whom he had deceived years earlier, and he was deeply afraid of the possibility of his brother seeking revenge. This fear triggered a night of solitude and reflection as Jacob contemplated his future and the consequences of his actions.

The wrestling match itself represents a deeper struggle beyond the physical confrontation. It symbolizes Jacob's lifelong battle with his identity, his desire for blessings, and his struggle with God's plans for his life. Throughout Jacob's life, he was known for relying on his ability to scheme and be cunning, as seen in his manipulation of both Esau and their father, Isaac. However, this night of wrestling revealed his internal conflict with God's authority and his need to be blessed and affirmed by God rather than by man.

By wrestling with God, Jacob was finally forced to confront the deeper spiritual issues in his life—his need for reconciliation, divine favor, and a relationship with God based on surrender rather than self-reliance.

From Angela

I live my life in tension. The tension between joy and suffering. I experience euphoric joy on a daily basis, and yet my life has been equally marked by deep suffering. I have an incredible and undeniable gift of faith. I have also wrestled with God through many nights. Only he and I know the extent and the depth to which we've wrestled. So how am I able to have a heart full of faith even as I emotionally flood the Lord with questions as to *why* he hasn't answered the one prayer I need answered?

We've all had moments where we call out to God with a deafening cry, expecting him to answer—and yet silence is what we receive. At other times, we see his hand move powerfully in response to our prayers. This contrast can be perplexing and painful and leaves us wondering: *Why does God answer some prayers but not others?* In those moments, we often find ourselves wrestling with God, like Jacob did, seeking an answer, a breakthrough, or even just understanding.

I have spent a great deal of my life praying for the people closest to me. I pray for healing, for freedom, for deliverance, and for the people I love to no longer live in a context of crisis and chaos but in the fullness of joy and peace that I know is available to them through Jesus. Have you ever prayed, "Lord, if you just answer this one, you never have to answer anything else again. Just this one prayer. Just this one healing. Just this one family member. Just this one miracle." And it's . . . radio silence. No movement. No change. I say, "But, God, you're still God. You're still good." (*But I am so mad at you.*) "But I believe without a shadow of a doubt that you are who you say you are." (*But you're hurting me.*)

This has been the greatest point of pain over the past ten years of my life, and it's gotten significantly more difficult the last few years of being all in with Jesus and in ministry. I believe in a miracle-working, on-the-spot-healing Jesus. I've seen *miracles.* I've seen God rewire my own brain, heal my mental health, and deliver me from multiple addictions. I watched him reverse lifelong trauma and depression in my best friend. I receive hundreds of testimonies *a day* from our audience telling us how Jesus is legitimately healing and saving them through our podcast.

And I, once again, still find myself in the tension. Countless precious souls are being saved by Jesus, but I can't bring that same power and healing into my own home. It stings. And it's confusing.

Deep, deep tension. Pulling at me from opposite directions. A wrestle in my heart. Gratitude and anger. Hope and despair. How can I so easily vacillate between these feelings?

I experienced a very interesting moment and perfect example of this tension recently. One night, after an intense fast with the intention for breakthrough for someone I love dearly, I got a call about this person. It wasn't good news. And it filled my heart with anxiety and confusion, because what were the chances that I would be fasting for him and he would be getting worse?

Simultaneously, I've been walking with one of my best friends in her faith journey for quite some time, and I've seen major breakthrough recently. She has gone all in with Jesus, and I get a front-row seat to watch the way she's discovering him and how he's encountering her. It's so beautiful and life-giving. And I have prayed so much for this to happen.

The very next morning after I received that call of bad news, my best friend called me to tell me how she'd prayed to God the night before that he would prove he was real by waking her up at 5 A.M.—and he did. He did it. He answered her prayer.

And it stung. He could answer that prayer. But he couldn't answer mine.

And I again found myself wrestling with God. I didn't know how to feel! I was so grateful he was coming through for my friend, but what about the matter that was causing me such an incredible amount of distress and despair? My heart was still full of faith, but I was also upset that there was no movement for my circumstance. No change! Still, even in my pain and anger, my heart was ablaze with fiery faith that Jesus is Lord, and I love him more every second that goes by. Amid excruciating pain, I proclaim that he is Lord because that's who he is. It is truth, and the truth does not bend or bow based on my circumstance.

If you're familiar with the Old Testament, you may have heard the word *lament*. To lament means to passionately express grief or sorrow. And I've realized recently that God is inviting me to lament. He's inviting me to wrestle. Wrestling with God is a natural part of a life of faith. He is not distant or uncaring. Wrestling in prayer is a testimony to the intimacy of our relationship with him. Trust me, he can handle it.

I love how in the book of Lamentations, the author and prophet, Jeremiah, conveyed polarizing emotions very similar to mine. He wrote, "My eyes fail from weeping, I am in torment within; my heart is poured out on the ground because my people are destroyed" (2:11). But then he went on to say, "Yet I still dare to hope when I remember this: The faithful love of the LORD never ends! His mercies never cease" (3:21–22, NLT).

And then Lamentations 5:19–22 (NLT) says:

> But LORD, you remain the same forever!
>> Your throne continues from generation to generation.
>>> [i.e., *faith*]
>
> Why do you continue to forget us?
>> Why have you abandoned us for so long? [i.e., *doubt*]
>
> Restore us, O LORD, and bring us back to you again!
>> Give us back the joys we once had! [i.e., *hope*]
>
> Or have you utterly rejected us?
>> Are you angry with us still? [i.e., *despair* and *distrust*]³

I've come to a beautiful point of acceptance that there may be some redemption I will not see on this side of eternity. It may only be when our earthly bodies have transferred and transformed into our heavenly bodies, where there is no mourning or sickness or pain, that I will receive my wish to see my loved ones healed.

I love the fact that after Jacob wrestled with God, he walked with a limp. I, too, find myself naturally walking with a limp—*one foot on earth and one foot in heaven*. Faith . . . and a lack of faith. Trust . . . and mistrust. Joy . . . and suffering. Profound strength . . . and profound weakness. All realities of journeying with God. The kingdom is so full of tension that reveals so much beauty through the human existence.

I don't want to offer you Christian clichés in an attempt to put a Band-Aid over your suffering. Even when it's well-intentioned, hearing that can be excruciating. But the truth is, God's wisdom transcends our limited view, and both his answers and his silence are expressions of his love. God's silence or delay often becomes a divine invitation to deeper dependence on him, an invitation to rest in his sovereign will, even when we don't understand it.

The life of faith is a continual process of wrestling with God, not in opposition to him, but in pursuit of a deeper relationship and understanding.

Dear Father,

I thank you for being a God who hears me, even when I don't understand your ways. Help me to trust you in both the answered and unanswered prayers. Give me the faith to wrestle with you in hope, the perseverance to hold on in the silence, and the grace to trust that your plans are always for my good.

In Jesus's name, amen.

Your turn: What have you learned about Jesus in this devotion, and how does this apply to your season in the wilderness?

_____

_____

_____

_____

_____

_____

Day Fourteen

The Bible: A Lamp to My Feet

In the beginning was the Word, and the Word was with God, and the Word was God. He was with God in the beginning. Through him all things were made; without him nothing was made that has been made. In him was life, and that life was the light of all mankind.

—John 1:1–4

I am the vine; you are the branches. If you remain in me and I in you, you will bear much fruit; apart from me you can do nothing.

—John 15:5

Your word is a lamp to my feet
and a light to my path.
—Psalm 119:105, esv

Imagine a dark world where confusion and uncertainty reign. Amid the darkness, Jesus exists as a beacon of radiant light, illuminating the path to truth, peace, and divine love.

In embracing the light of Jesus, we find not only a guide for our earthly journey but also the assurance of eternal life. His light brings warmth to our hearts, clarity to our minds, and direction to our steps. It is a light that never fades, leading us ever closer to the heart of God.

Psalm 119:105 is one of our favorite verses because it sums up the whole Bible: *His Word is our light.* There is a reason why Jesus wants us to live a certain way. It's not to punish us but to free us. It is why when we try to live by our own rules, we experience depression and anxiety. But when we walk in the will of God, we walk in the fruit of the Spirit: love, joy, peace, patience, kindness, goodness, faithfulness, gentleness, and self-control.

From Arielle

Before I opened the Bible, I was just a girl searching for peace, trying to get by on my own strength. Doing so was painful and mentally exhausting, to say the least. I was constantly trying to navigate life and do the right thing, yet I always felt lost. Finally, I came to a dead end in my life. No doctor, therapist, or friend could cure me of the mental and emotional pain I was enduring. I was desperate to get better, but I was out of resources. This was when Angela told me we'd start reading the Bible together daily. She knew this would be the cure I was looking for.

That next morning, Angela started reading the book of John with me. But before reading each day, she would pray that we would receive interpretation and understanding of the Scriptures, that the Holy Spirit would reveal what God was trying to show us.

"In the beginning was the Word, and the Word was with God, and the Word was God," it began. *The Word is God,* I thought. *This book contains God's words.* Before this I didn't appreciate what the Bible was. I knew it was a book with stories, but I didn't understand its significance or value. Now I realize the Bible is more than a book. It is the unfolding revelation of Jesus.

When we got to John 8, Angela read, "When Jesus spoke again to the people, he said, 'I am the light of the world. Whoever follows me will never walk in darkness, but will have the light of life'" (verse 12). I felt like a little girl again, so curious and excited about the Bible. I asked Ang to explain what it meant.

She said, "This darkness that you're walking in, you won't have to walk in it anymore. God is the light of life. This Bible is the light of life. And when we read his promises and apply them and follow him, we will be in the light and no longer in the darkness."

Tears started streaming down my face.

Then she read John 15:5: "I am the vine; you are the branches. If you remain in me and I in you, you will bear much fruit; apart from me you can do nothing." She explained that without a connection to Christ, we cannot bear fruit or live a fruitful life.

It was all making sense—the darkness, confusion, and hopelessness I felt. My eyes were opened to the truth for the first time in my life. Angela looked at me, a smile on her face. "You look different. There's light in your eyes," she said.

And she was right; this was the point my life began moving from darkness to light. Though I was still in a time of transition and healing, I knew who I was doing it with. Instead of going by my own strength, I had something to stand on and trust: the Word of God.

The words on those pages were instilling life in me. It was medicine to my spirit. I was reading about Jesus's nature, and from beginning to end, it showed him meeting the needs of his people. I was learning about how he keeps every single one of his promises and how he's always right on time. His Word had an answer for every situation. It was teaching me how to be right with him. His unconditional love, mercy, miracles, care, and gentleness brought safety to my life that I had never had before.

It was humbling to learn how he sacrificed for us—coming down from heaven to take on human flesh, consciously limiting himself—and what he'd had to endure—betrayal, brutal torture, being hung between two thieves and executed on a cross while wearing a crown of thorns. By sacrificing himself for us on the cross, he took the punishment for all our sins. All for us.

Before I read the Bible, I was experiencing who he was by what he was doing through my life and my own personal intimacy with him. But when I actually read his words and discovered the depths of what he went through for us, I began to really understand the profundity of who my Father was.

I had struggled my whole life with obsessive-compulsive thinking, and negative thoughts had always plagued me. But suddenly I found that I was becoming peace-filled and the disturbing voices in my head were subsiding. Reading the Bible helped to completely renew my mind. John 8:31–32 says, "If you hold to my teaching, you are really my disciples. Then you will know the truth, and the truth will set you free."

I started taking my unwanted thoughts captive and replacing them with Jesus's words. I trusted him with all my heart, knowing that he works all things together for my good. I knew I could not lean on my own understanding and that in all things, he would make my path straight. The Bible taught me to walk by faith and not by sight, and God revealed to me the areas in my life that I needed to change, which wasn't easy to face. But with God's help, I put my pride aside and faced my weaknesses. This process taught me repentance and restored my fellowship with him. It led me to salvation and taught me how to live a holy life—not a perfect life, but one of obedience. When I started applying his commandments, that's when life drastically changed for the better. I felt like I had cracked the code to a life of fulfillment.

I want you to know that every single word he speaks is for our benefit. God makes no mistakes. I am so passionate about this because life can be so difficult. If everyone could understand that God designed his Word the way he did so that we can live in the light, our world would be much different. We all want to be healed and live in joy. And guess what? We have access to that! It's all in his Word, the Bible. God has also given us the Bible to serve him and to share with others.

This is the divine revelation of the Almighty God, given to us to live by, to discover who he is and what he's like, and to show us how we can live every single day knowing in our hearts that we have a security that is divinely given. He wants to teach us what life is all about and how we can spend eternity with him.

Dear Father,

I love you, Lord. I pray you would teach me how to abide in you and you in me. Lord, I ask you to teach me to live my life as you would have me live it, in total dependence upon you (which is the life of Christ being lived through me), so that I may produce the good fruit in my life that is honoring to you. Help me to read and receive revelation through your Word. Thank you for all you do for me, Lord. Thank you for being a Father who comforts and protects and loves the way you do.

In Jesus's name, amen.

Your turn: What have you learned about Jesus in this devotion, and how does this apply to your season in the wilderness?

The One True God

You shall have no other gods before me.

 You shall not make for yourself a carved image, or any likeness of anything that is in heaven above, or that is in the earth beneath, or that is in the water under the earth. You shall not bow down to them or serve them, for I the LORD your God am a jealous God.
—EXODUS 20:3–5, ESV

Do not turn to idols or make metal gods for yourselves. I am the LORD your God.
—LEVITICUS 19:4

Our God displays covenant-level loyalty. But he expects the same from us in return. He's jealous for us, and he makes it very clear in his Word that we are not to worship any other "gods." The worship of the one true God is the only appropriate belief and practice we are to have as followers of Christ. To worship an idol means to worship someone or something other than God as though it were God, and today this can happen in a variety of ways. You can outright worship or believe in a false god, believe in a practice that taps into the spiritual realm outside the will and authority of Jesus Christ, or even give inanimate objects God-like characteristics.

 Worshipping idols is not only sinful but incredibly dangerous. And if I were the devil, I would do exactly what he's done and still does. He takes something harmful and evil and puts it in a beautiful package of "light," then calls it manifestation, chakra alignment, crystal healing, tarot, spirit guides, psychics, witchcraft, astrology, and so much more. Even Satan worship has become trendy and cute somehow. The push to use psychedelic drugs to tap into one's spiritual life has become so normalized it's frightening. These are all dangerous practices that are being embraced in our modern culture, and we must be aware in order to protect ourselves and guard our hearts.

From Angela

When I moved into my house in Hollywood, I was probably only a month into reading my Bible. I was *so* in love with Jesus, but there was still a lot of work he had to do in me. To give a little context, I got sober when I was twenty-three and started reading the Bible when I was twenty-five. In the two years in between, I was focused on developing my prayer life and learning about the authority I had through Jesus. In fact, I had become a little prayer warrior. But my lack of knowledge of the Word definitely left me in the dark about a lot of things I continued to allow in my life. So while I had a strong and growing relationship with Jesus, I was still heavily focused on meditation, breath work, and lighting sage and palo santo as a means of "cleansing energy."

One day during this period I walked into a little "magic" shop by my house to pick up incense. It was full of thousands of different potion oils (*Wanna get someone to fall in love with you? Hurt someone who hurt you? Get the guy who left you back?*), little statues of "gods" for different purposes (*Prosperity! Health! Abundance!*), candles that had powers (*Book the job! Make a million dollars! Get everything you've ever wanted!*), and so much more.

Doesn't it all sound great?

I mean, it really does. It *sounds* so positive and beneficial and "light." Yet 2 Corinthians 11:14–15 cautions us, "And no wonder, for Satan himself masquerades as an angel of light. It is not surprising, then, if his servants also masquerade as servants of righteousness." Yes, these things that sound so attractive are from the devil. Have you heard the saying "If you make a deal with the devil, the devil always comes knocking"? This is not a cliché. Nothing is free with that loser. Can Satan make wonderful things happen? Of course he can. But it always comes at a price. God's blessings are free. Do you see the difference between making a deal with the devil and making a deal with Jesus? You pay a price with Satan, but Jesus paid the price *for you*. Jesus tells us in John 10:10 that the thief (Satan) comes only to steal, kill, and destroy, but he—Jesus—came that we may have life and have it abundantly.

While I was looking around the shop, I passed a table with a bunch of little statues of gods with different purposes. I went to pick up one that was supposed to bring prosperity and financial blessing. As I was reaching for it, a wave of strong conviction flowed through me, stopping me abruptly. I didn't hear the audible voice of God, but I heard him unmistakably in my heart say, *No. That is not for you.* This was the first time I remember ever consciously hearing God's voice. It was a feeling and a type of conviction that hit me right there in the middle of that store. In an instant, I saw clearly behind the mask that New Age hides, preaching love and light but hiding the extreme darkness of the things in the shop. I left and never returned. I also went home and threw away any crystal, sage, and evil-eye pendants I had in my home.

My heart is absolutely crushed for all the people in the world who are in pain and desperate for answers, leaving them vulnerable and susceptible for Satan to feed off their desperation. These New Age practices only lead to more pain, suffering, confusion, and hopelessness. I promise I'm not here to judge you if you've participated in these practices, but the wholeness and fulfillment you're desperately searching for won't be found in any crystal or manifestation—that kind of healing can only be found in Jesus. I have only compassion in my heart for anyone involved in New Age spirituality. You know why? Because we're spiritual beings. We are innately spiritual. New Age devotees' inclination to feed themselves spiritually is beautiful, healthy, and natural—but they've been deceived into believing that the spiritual connection they're searching for is found in worldly things, and they are being fed by evil.

You don't need things of this world to bring you clarity, healing, or hope. Your hope rests in Jesus, the beginning and end of all things.

Dear Jesus,
Jesus Christ of Nazareth. Lord of lords. King of kings. The Alpha and Omega. The beginning and end. You are Lord above all, the one true living God. I repent from any time I have ever created an idol and put something above you or before you. If I have been involved in any occult, witchcraft, or demonic activity, knowingly or unknowingly, I renounce and reject this behavior and I ask for your forgiveness. I ask that you take your rightful place on the throne as Lord of my life. I exalt you high above every other thing. My heart belongs to you alone. I love you.
In your name I pray, amen.

Your turn: What have you learned about Jesus in this devotion, and how does this apply to your season in the wilderness?

Day Sixteen

From Addiction to Breakthrough

Come to me, all of you who are tired from carrying heavy loads, and I will give you rest. Take my yoke and put it on you, and learn from me, because I am gentle and humble in spirit; and you will find rest.

—Matthew 11:28–29, GNT

Have you ever been burdened with distress or guilt be-cause of a mistake you've made? Have you ever experienced hopelessness and shame because you keep making the same mistake? Maybe you're dealing with an addiction, and you can't see how you will ever overcome it. Maybe you've wondered if you're even worth it, or whether the effort of overcoming the addiction is worth it. The cost feels too great, and you genuinely don't know if you can bear it any longer.

But we're not meant to carry our burdens alone.

No matter what you're carrying or facing, remember this: God's got you and will not let you go. In him you can rest. You are not your addiction or your season of drought. Through Christ, all things are possible, and you can overcome what's weighing you down.

When God allows you to experience opposition, he's offering an opportunity to show you who you really are. When God shakes things up, he's trying to shake you up to change you for the better. And when God strips away some of the bad habits or addictions in your life, he's calling you to receive something better.

From Arielle

I always thank God for my dad. He is the hero of heroes, and his heart is pure gold. When I was younger, he was the light of my world—and still is. Even as a single parent, he did everything he could to give me the best life. He worked overtime seven days a week to provide for us and never complained, not even once. He would come home with a bag full of groceries, ready to make home-cooked meals together as though he hadn't worked all day. He spent all his free time with me, going on adventures, playing with me, taking me to the mall and pretending he actually liked helping me pick out makeup, and teaching me new recipes. He played the role of mom, dad, and best friend all in one.

At his job as a car salesman, he would sometimes take me to work with him and let me pretend to be a receptionist. On other days, he would get home late but hide his exhaustion with a smile and then take me for ice cream so we could sit and talk about my day. Whenever I was going through a rough time, he would take me for long car rides until I felt okay again. He was strong, selfless, understanding, and always so supportive—my friend when I had none. He was also cheerful, with a childlike spirit that made everyone love him.

But then something changed.

When I was sixteen, my dad came home from work with something different about him. The brightness in his eyes had turned to darkness.

"Dad, are you okay?" I asked.

"Yeah, honey, just tired."

He quietly went into his room and stayed there.

Over the next few months, his nine-to-nine workdays turned into nine to two in the morning. The cheerful "How was your day?" and "Let's go on a drive!" greetings turned into silence and an inability to look me in the eyes. And it only got worse. Eventually, when he would stumble into the house each night, it was clear I was invisible to him. I had lost my dad mentally and emotionally, and it broke my heart.

Our relationship reached a tipping point one Sunday morning when I came out into the living room and found Dad shivering, pale, and rocking back and forth.

"Dad? Are you cold?"

He couldn't answer.

I wrapped a blanket around him and held him. Then, breaking down into a panic, I called the paramedics, terrified he was dying. It took thirty minutes for them to arrive, and I spent the entire time in anguish, watching my dad in this derailed state.

When the paramedics did come, they told me he had relapsed—a shock to me, since I hadn't been aware he'd ever had substance issues. As I watched him get carried out, my safety, along with my heart, felt like it had been ripped away from me.

My hero, the one who always acted like everything was fine, was far from okay.

I found out later that the years of taking on overnight shifts, suppressing his own feelings, and abandoning himself to care for me had led to him hitting a wall. A wall that turned him to drinking and pills.

Thankfully, he went to rehab and got sober, and a month after that, it felt like I had my dad back.

Later that year I moved to Los Angeles to pursue my career. But before I left I asked him, "Dad, will you be okay?"

"Yeah, honey. You're a good kid. Don't ever forget it," he said in his Boston accent. (That was our saying.)

I was working at a restaurant in L.A. when I got the call. It was my dad—from jail. He had been drunk driving and had hit a tree. The result was a DUI, with his license being suspended for four years. I can still feel the way my heart dropped. I knew my dad had made mistakes, but I had thought he was better.

My dad had gone from being a strong, resilient man to being broken, lost, and suicidal. He told me he couldn't get through it alone this time.

We decided he should come to sunny L.A. and start fresh in a place where we could be together. I remember thinking what a gift it was that he hadn't taken his life, and that I could give back and help him the way he'd always helped me.

It definitely wasn't easy.

Over the next four years, I watched as he was stripped of everything. He went from being my self-sufficient dad to becoming someone who needed me to take care of him emotionally, which was extremely tough since I could barely take care of myself at the time. I could tell he was ashamed that he was no longer the man and father he had always been.

One day, I decided to take him on a long drive like he had always done for me. The conversation we had turned into a breakthrough.

"Dad, remember when you could barely take care of yourself because you had to take care of me, and you did it with a smile on your face? Or when, at all my school plays and milestones, you were the only one there, always sitting in the front row cheering me on? Or at Christmas, how you would get up extra early and wait for me to wake up so you could watch me open presents? Or how much peace and safety you gave me daily by playing the role of a mom and dad all in one? I look back on my childhood, and I have so many joyful memories because of you."

I could see the light returning to his eyes again.

"I love you, Dad. You're strong, and you're my hero. We'll get through this together."

That next year, my dad devoted himself to attending AA and to reading and learning the Bible, which led him to a place of rest and peace. He's been sober for seven years now, and he is stronger than he ever was. Better yet, his life is better than it ever was. Even more incredible is that, through his struggle and hardship, he now coaches and helps others who are battling addiction. His own addiction, sorrow, and hardship allowed him to become wiser and better. The challenges we faced together proved to be blessings in disguise. For through them, we grew so much together, and God showed me that sometimes things need to fall apart before they can fall together.

Father,

I reach out to you as I navigate this path of addiction and recovery. I stand here, vulnerable yet determined, seeking your guidance and strength. I wrestle with my past choices, and I yearn for the light of your healing to touch my soul. I humbly come before you, seeking your divine intervention to break the chains of addiction that bind me. I am reaching out to those who understand my struggles and am seeking companions on this challenging path.

With each passing day, grant me the clarity to see the beauty of my pain. Show me the path to self-discovery and self-love, where the void left by addiction and depression can be filled with self-worth. I ask for your unwavering presence. Lift me when I stumble, Lord; hold me when the enticement of my old habits calls; and celebrate me in the moments of victory, no matter how small.

Amen.

Your turn: What have you learned about Jesus in this devotion, and how does this apply to your season in the wilderness?

_____

_____

_____

_____

_____

_____

_____

_____

_____

_____

_____

_____

Don't Go Back to the Very Thing God Delivered You From

Because your men explored the land for forty days, you must wander in the wilderness for forty years—a year for each day, suffering the consequences of your sins. Then you will discover what it is like to have me for an enemy.
—Numbers 14:34, NLT

After God had assigned Moses to help free his people from Egypt, Moses was then selected to lead the Israelites to Canaan, the Promised Land. But after hearing bad reports from the men sent ahead to spy on the land, the Israelites grumbled about Moses's and Aaron's leadership. Despite the miracles they'd witnessed firsthand, the people rebelled against God. Many said they wished they had died in Egypt, and some even suggested choosing a leader to take them back to the land where they'd been enslaved.

However, Joshua and Caleb, two of the scouts sent into Canaan, were faithful to the Lord. They encouraged the people to put their faith in God and believe that he would empower them to conquer the land. But the people threatened to stone them.

As a result of the Israelites' disobedience and lack of faith, God punished Israel, and they were forced to wander in the wilderness for forty years, until all the people of the older generation had died. None of them—not even Moses—would ever enter the Promised Land, except for Caleb and Joshua, whose faith God rewarded.

From Angela

A few years ago, I got into an unhealthy relationship. Only three months in, I saw that the relationship had become very controlling and was on its way to becoming downright toxic. It hadn't gotten there yet, but the writing was on the wall. I saw it, and I heard God asking me to trust him.

So I listened. Acting in obedience to God, I ended the relationship.

Unfortunately, I couldn't stick to my decision. Since I was very isolated in my faith, I wasn't strong enough to stay away from the toxic guy. I felt lonely and anxious and missed him terribly, so I took him back. Instead of my loneliness driving me to God, I bought into the lie that God couldn't provide the comfort, love, and confidence I needed. Adversity had hit, and in the heat of the moment, I surrendered to my flesh.

So I rebelled against God out of an arrogant belief that I could control the outcome. The guy and I got back together, but the relationship continued to turn toxic, eventually becoming far worse than I could've imagined.

I spent the next six months in what felt like hell because I'd chosen to ignore God. Because I didn't trust God's will for my life, what could have been six months of discovering a stronger relationship with Jesus and developing my faith became six months of sadness, uncertainty, and fear.

If I'd been faithful, if I'd truly surrendered and laid down the relationship the first time, I would have been saved from massive heartache.

I thought God was taking something from me by encouraging me to break up with the guy, but I now realize he could see the outcome. He could see the six months of suffering and didn't want me to experience that. He wanted to protect me from it. Instead, I picked the relationship back up as a quick fix to my problems, and my disobedience and lack of faith led to more pain and the need for healing.

I am a firm believer in God's peace. In fact, I don't just believe in it—I depend on it. And I believe a lack of peace is evidence of a misalignment with God's will. Many times, the peace of God has given me confidence to step out in faith even when I was scared. Similarly, the lack of God's peace has saved me from things that would have caused total chaos in my life. Whenever I'm making any decision, I look for God's peace or the absence of it. Jesus is the Prince of Peace, while the devil is the author of confusion. Maybe you've heard it said before, but you'll know something is from God if it comes with peace. You'll know it's not when it comes with confusion, anxiety, chaos, and unrest.

My heart aches for those who stay in unhealthy relationships—including my younger self—even when all the signs are screaming *leave*. There may be numerous reasons why we stay in these less-than-God's-best-for-us situations. Perhaps we grew up in an environment where a certain behavior was normal, and we allow this type of behavior from our significant other because it's simply all we know. But one of my favorites of God's promises—and a practice of the Christian faith—is the renewal of the mind.

According to Romans 12:2, renewing your mind means interpreting life through the lens of God's Word and the inspiration of the Holy Spirit, rather than through the lens of your experience, trauma, upbringing, or societal influences. I believe that God is a God of renewal, and he has the ability to rewire our brains and untangle even the most deeply ingrained toxic behaviors. I know from experience that he will replace unhealthy thought patterns with healthy, godly ones. And he does that through intimacy with him and with his Word. The Bible is full of truths that are applicable to your life in any given circumstance.

Studying his Word and learning the truth is what absolutely changed my life. I would never allow things now that I would when I was younger. For example, now I know what love is, in God's eyes. And it's certainly not controlling, toxic, or chaotic.

The Bible says in 1 Corinthians 13:4–7, "Love is patient, love is kind. It does not envy, it does not boast, it is not proud. It does not dishonor others, it is not self-seeking, it is not easily angered, it keeps no record of wrongs. Love does not delight in evil but rejoices with the truth. It always protects, always trusts, always hopes, always perseveres."

I pray for every single one of my dear friends in situations like the one I described. And I pray that God divinely intercedes and has his way in your situation. You are stronger than you think. And just because you've lived your whole life accepting certain behaviors does not mean you have to continue. I have so much faith in you and the God that is in you.

Dear Jesus,

First, I want to say that I'm sorry. I'm sorry for every single time I rebel against you. I'm sorry for every time I hear your voice and choose to ignore it. I don't want to be like the Israelites, prolonging their wilderness season due to their lack of faith.

Lord, give me the wisdom to discern your will for my life. Give me the strength and maturity to submit to it. May your will be done in my life, as it is in heaven. If I step out of your will, Good Shepherd, guide me back onto your path. I also pray that you aid in the renewal of my mind. Rewire my thought patterns to think thoughts only through the lens of your Word. May I only accept a love that is pleasing in your eyes. Show me what love is. I love you, Jesus. Thank you for your perfect will.

In your name I pray, amen.

Your turn: What have you learned about Jesus in this devotion, and how does this apply to your season in the wilderness?

_____

_____

_____

_____

_____

_____

_____

_____

_____

_____

_____

Day Eighteen

His Timeline, Not Mine

You do not understand now what I am doing, but you will understand later.
—JOHN 13:7, GNT

We know that in all things God works for the good of those who love him, who have been called according to his purpose.
—ROMANS 8:28

There is a time for everything,
and a season for every activity under the heavens.
—ECCLESIASTES 3:1

We love to do things in our own timing. Eager for all the good things, we often try to jump ahead and do things our way. And if what we want doesn't happen, we get impatient with God.

But God allows different seasons for a reason, and we might miss out on his plans if we try to skip any of them. Maybe your current wilderness season involves singleness. This isn't because God wants to withhold good things from you. He wants to build trust with you and to create an intimate relationship where he is first in your life. If you experience hard circumstances or challenges in your wilderness season, he wants you to come to him instead of running to other people or comforts of the world. Because he loves you and wants to build something in you, he is using this time to prepare you to step into whatever new season he has in store for you next.

From Arielle

I often heard how fun singleness could be, but no one prepared me for how much of a shock it would be for someone who was used to always being in a relationship. When I entered a season of singleness for the first time, let's just say it was the furthest thing from fun. Or easy.

As someone who desires to be a wife and a mother and who adored every second of being in a relationship, being suddenly single was beyond difficult. It was unsettling to go from having someone there through all my wins and losses—protecting me and loving me—to being completely alone. It felt like a literal blow to my nervous system. Not to mention, I then felt like I was constantly watching all my friends plan their weddings, move into their homes with their spouses, go on date nights, and plan their baby reveals. As happy as I was for them, I couldn't help falling into a pit of bitterness, thinking, *God, why isn't this happening for me? Will it even happen for me? Is my person ever coming?* These thoughts were followed by feelings of unworthiness because I no longer had that sense of love and affection from my person.

Maybe you can relate.

When my long-term relationship ended, I spent months on my hands and knees begging and bargaining with God to bring it back. I wrestled with him day and night, angry, frustrated, and confused about why I had to be in this position. It felt like I was being punished in some way.

Little did I know, the break from relationships was far from a punishment. Singleness proved to be a *gift* God had given me.

Over time, I started to realize I was wasting my days looking back. I didn't want to keep drowning in my heartache or barely functioning in the blur of autopilot. There had to be more to life than this. There had to be more than this sinking feeling of emptiness.

As I stopped complaining and started trusting more in God, I noticed he was working something in me that on my best day I could not do on my own. So I submitted and surrendered to the process. Slowly, God revealed that I had been giving everything to my relationship and had totally abandoned myself along the way. Now that I was single, I had to identify what my heart really needed: love, peace, and hope. Instead of chasing a guy for those things, I began finding them in Jesus. Instead of attaching my worth to another person, I recognized that a relationship with God was what my heart and soul needed. Instead of searching for a boyfriend to complete me, I discovered that only Jesus could ever truly satisfy me.

What a miracle that I met God during my singleness season, right?

After undergoing this divine transformation and renewal of my mind, I completely devoted myself to God's work. I knew that God needed me to be his bride before I could be one to anyone else. So I made a promise to him and myself that I would use the time of singleness to make myself the absolute best version of who I could be. Realizing I already had my Savior, I stopped waiting for someone to sweep me off my feet. And even while my friends were getting married and having kids, I stopped wishing for those things and started building my own life.

When I did, my life radically changed in the best way.

I found my purpose—my pride and joy—with *Girls Gone Bible.* I built the most incredible friendships, traveled to new and exciting places, and built memories I used to dream of having. For the first time, I got to see myself for who I really was: capable, worthy, smart, and valuable.

I was able to go on a journey of becoming whole as a woman, having realized that if I did not know how to be satisfied in my singleness, then I would never be satisfied in any relationship. If romantic love was my highest goal, I would always feel empty and desperate. If my only aim was a relationship, then I would always be disappointed and hurt. Only Jesus could fill the void in my life and satisfy the longing in my soul.

And the same is true for you too.

As frustrating and hard as it can be, singleness also offers us a time to discover and grow who we are and to ask the question, *God, who have you called me to be?* If we ignore or avoid questions like that and fail to find out who we are, it will complicate our relational identity. Without a good grasp on who we are when we enter into relationships, we will try to bend to fit the other person's needs and expectations, because we lack understanding of who *we* are and what *we* need.

In my time of singleness, I have seen miracles and learned to trust God instead of panicking. I have learned never to question his motives, even when circumstances look dark and don't make sense. Even in those times, God whispers, *It's okay. Trust me. I'm still working in you, and I'm not done yet.* As John 13:7 says, "You do not understand now what I am doing, but you will understand later" (GNT).

Maybe you still don't understand why God has you in this season right now. Maybe all you can see is the hurt and confusion. But I want to encourage you to see your season of singleness as a sign not of abandonment but of God's love. As something designed and intentional to prepare you for your future, beyond temporary happiness.

God is never in a hurry and he is never late. His timing is always perfect. If it seems like he's late, just know that he's actually getting you ready for a miracle. So do not fear. Time is not running out, and you are right on track. He is working it out.

Dear God,

Thank you for your presence in my life. Thank you for each and every season you place before me. In this time of singleness, please draw me closer to you and teach me how to lean on you alone. Teach me to always turn to you, to put my hope, faith, and trust in you, and to know that your timing is always perfect. Help me to release any stress or anxiety and embrace your peace, knowing that you work all things for our good, that you are building something new in me, and that you are with me. I love you, Father.

In Jesus's name, amen.

Your turn: What have you learned about Jesus in this devotion, and how does this apply to your season in the wilderness?

Power in the Name

I have given you authority to trample on snakes and scorpions and
to overcome all the power of the enemy; nothing will harm you.
—Luke 10:19

When Jesus addressed the seventy-two disciples he sent
out on mission to preach and heal, he said, "I have given you authority."
This authority was a divine empowerment to carry out their mission
and to defeat any dangerous or evil forces of the enemy. As the disciples
prepared to go, Jesus gave them a promise of protection, reassuring
them that they would be safeguarded from harm.

Even though Jesus spoke those words in a distant time and place,
this verse emphasizes the authority and protection given to all Jesus's
followers—including those of us today. Our relationship with Jesus
gives us power. This power enables us to confront and overcome evil as
we carry out our divine mission.

From Angela

We have an enemy, and his name is Satan. He is a real being whose pri-
mary desire is to oppose God and his plans, and to deceive and destroy

humanity. He hates when we draw close to God, and he will do anything to keep us isolated and hopeless.

The most intense way the devil came for me was by attacking my mental health. From the age of nineteen to twenty-four, I struggled with severe anxiety. And when I say "struggle," I mean anxiety had its foot on my neck. During that horrible time, the devil did everything in his power to ensure I never knew my authority through or identity in Jesus. He distracted me and discouraged me. He whispered the lie that I was worthless. He made me feel alone.

But the second I opened my Bible and discovered the revelation of who Jesus is—who my *Lord* really is—it was over. Anxiety went from standing on my neck to cowering under my feet. All it took was the revelation of the *authority* given to me by Jesus.

I'm so passionate about speaking on this topic because I see so many people who even as followers of Jesus fall victim to the schemes of the devil. For many of them, they have allowed fear to replace the revelation of who Jesus is as Lord, King, and Champion. (This doesn't include people who suffer from clinical depression and other mental illnesses.) They have forgotten that, as followers of Christ, we don't fight *for* victory, but *from* a place of victory because of the finished work on the cross. They need to remember that we are champions because of the one who champions us. As Romans 8:37 says, "No, in all these things we are more than conquerors through him who loved us."

When I began fighting my anxiety with the words of Scripture, I quickly learned about the supernatural power granted to me by the precious blood of the Lamb. Revelation caught; devil defeated. Because of Jesus's sacrifice on the cross, I realized that nothing on earth has dominion over me. It is all subject to the authority of Jesus—an authority I can call on anytime. I started to *speak* to the anxiety, commanding it to go back to hell where it came from by the *authority* given to me through the *name of Jesus*. I cast out the spirit of anxiety and panic every time it came up, and because I believed in the promise God gave me, it worked. It continues to work today and bring miraculous transformation to my life.

Amazingly, this authority is not the only power believers have from God. He has given us a holy arsenal of tools we can use every day:

The Holy Spirit—All believers have the power to overcome sin in their lives through the transformative work of the Holy Spirit, which enables us to resist sinful behaviors and live in accordance with God's will (Romans 6:14).

I was a lukewarm Christian before letting the Holy Spirit empower me to step away from my sinful behaviors. Now I rely on the authority I receive from Jesus to resist temptation when it arises. With his power, I am much more able to withstand temptation.

Spiritual armor—As we find several times throughout the Bible, believers are granted authority over demonic influences and evil spirits. This is evident in many accounts when Jesus and his disciples cast out demons (Mark 16:17; Luke 10:17).

For my part, I believe in casting out demons today the same way the disciples did in the Bible. I don't care if modern Christianity deems it overly spiritual. I know I've been able to cast demonic spirits out of myself and others, for the glory of God and the benefit of his people. Scripture says Jesus "appointed twelve of them and called them his apostles. They were to accompany him, and he would send them out to preach, giving them authority to cast out demons" (Mark 3:14–15, NLT). To ignore this God-given gift to perform deliverance is to miss out on the power he has given us.

Healing—The New Testament describes many instances when Jesus's followers performed miraculous healings. This suggests that believers can pray for, and sometimes witness, divine healing—both physically and spiritually (James 5:14–16).

I also believe in being able to pray for miraculous healings in the name of Jesus today. When Peter healed a man who was lame from birth, he said, "Silver or gold I do not have, but what I do have I give you. In the name of Jesus Christ of Nazareth, walk" (Acts 3:6). The power to heal is something we can all pray for as believers of Jesus.

Proclamation of the gospel—The Holy Spirit empowers believers to boldly share the message of salvation through Jesus Christ. This involves both the courage to speak and the wisdom to articulate the gospel effectively (Acts 1:8; Matthew 28:19–20).

I use the authority given to me by Jesus by spreading the gospel. My best friend, Ari, and I are the last people on earth who should have a platform to preach about Jesus. But through Jesus, by his power and his Spirit, we are able to communicate the gospel in a way that is impactful and effective, despite being unqualified and unequipped. It is not we who speak, but God in us. It is by his power and grace that we are unashamed to preach the Word of God, on any platform, in front of any audience.

Prayer—Believers have the privilege of prayer, which allows us to communicate with God, seek his guidance, intercede for others, and experience his peace. Jesus taught that prayer in his name carries significant power (John 14:13–14; James 5:16).

Prayer is one of the most significant parts of my faith. I pray like I breathe, as if my life depends on it. Because it does. Interceding with prayer is one of the most powerful tools God has given us, because it offers direct access to him. Prayer is so supernatural it can bend reality and change the outcome of a situation. All in the powerful name of Jesus.

Enduring trials—Jesus did not promise believers an easy path, but he did promise to give us strength to endure hardships and trials with hope, perseverance, and resilience—all while being rooted in our faith in Christ, who is always with us (2 Corinthians 12:9–10; Philippians 4:13).

The power and authority given to me by Jesus is my life raft and anchor in the storm. It is what gives me the ability to keep my head above water when I am drowning in the trials of life. Jesus never said the storms wouldn't come, but he promises to be in the boat with us, and he grants us the power to endure. Although the storms may rage, his power offers us peace, joy, and hope through it all.

Dear Father,

I come before you with a humble heart. You are the creator of the heavens and the earth, and all power and authority belong to you.

Lord, I ask for your divine authority in my life. Grant me the strength and courage to stand firm against the schemes of the enemy. Empower me with your Holy Spirit so that I may walk in the fullness of the authority you have given to your children. Help me to speak your truth boldly and to act in accordance with your will. Let your wisdom guide my decisions and your love shape my actions.

May your Word be a lamp to my feet and a light to my path, giving me the clarity and confidence to exercise the authority you have entrusted to me. Let your will be done in my life, as it is in heaven. I love you, Father.

In the mighty name of Jesus I pray, amen.

Your turn: What have you learned about Jesus in this devotion, and how does this apply to your season in the wilderness?

_____

_____

_____

_____

_____

_____

_____

_____

Day Twenty

Love Came Down
and He Rescued Me

After this, Jesus traveled about from one town and village to another, proclaiming the good news of the kingdom of God. The Twelve were with him, and also some women who had been cured of evil spirits and diseases: Mary (called Magdalene) from whom seven demons had come out.
—Luke 8:1–2

One can only speculate what it was like when Jesus looked upon Mary Magdalene in her state of desperation. Only he could have seen who she really was at her worst moment. After Jesus commanded the demons to leave her, Mary became a woman of strong faith. Her desperate longing to be close to Christ and serve him became how she lived her life. With unwavering loyalty, she supported the early Christian church as one of the few prominent female followers of Jesus. Her story serves as an example of faith and dedication, and she remains an important figure in Christianity today.

From Arielle

As with Mary Magdalene, mental health issues had taken over my mind and life. I often couldn't even recognize who I was looking at in the mirror. Anxiety, depression, and obsessive-compulsive thoughts had become part of my identity. Living with anxiety was like being followed by a voice that knew all my insecurities and used them against me. Eventually, it became the loudest voice in the room, the only one I could hear.

My beautiful mom suffered severely with mental health issues. Eventually, her struggle became so difficult that she didn't want to leave her room. As a result, I would deny what I was feeling and going through internally. I fought hard to be okay and grasped for peace. I would obsess and fixate on things so much that I would ask the same repetitive questions over and over again, beat myself up, self-blame, and find myself dwelling on a topic to the point of it completely taking over my mind. It left me crippled with anxiety every day.

Eventually, I put my shame to the side and mustered up the courage to go to a doctor, in the hope that I would hear some words of comfort about the way I was feeling or find a solution.

I asked the doctor, "Do you think I have a chance at beating this?"

She said, "Well, journaling, exercising, and meditation will help, but unfortunately, it's in your bloodline, so typically it only gets worse as you get older. But with medication, it can subside."

I felt defeated. I thought, *If this gets any worse, I don't know how I'll make it out alive. I'm already in survival mode.*

In 2021, my depression became so severe that the thought of dying became the only thing that calmed me. Death usually terrifies the average person, yet for me it felt like some sort of solution. My mind became a war zone that I couldn't escape. Intrusive thoughts screamed self-hatred at me, and I ruminated to the point that I finally gave in to taking medication that would help me sleep. Unfortunately, this only led to me feeling ten times worse when I woke up, because I was stuck with the same problems and no solution.

I became disconnected from myself and the world around me. People would try to talk to me, but it was like I couldn't hear what they were saying. I was completely dissociated. The shower became my safe place, and I would huddle there with the water beating down on my face, my hands over my head, pleading and begging for the intrusive thoughts to stop. My soul was tired, yet my mind wouldn't let me sleep. My life was passing me by.

"Get up, wipe your eyes, and enjoy the sunshine!" people said.

But even on the warmest, brightest day, I felt like I was in such darkness. I didn't see a way out.

As I mentioned earlier, a turning point came when I met Angela. I hadn't started reading the Bible yet, but Angela suggested we watch a show called *The Chosen,* an American historical television drama about the life of Jesus of Nazareth. It is based on the four books of the Bible known as the Gospels, which each tell the story of Jesus's life on earth from a different perspective. The night we watched the first episode is one I will never forget.

As a very visual person, I became completely enamored with watching the life of Jesus play out, but there was a specific scene that changed me that night—the story of Mary Magdalene. I saw how she suffered, how she was tortured by her thoughts, and how no one could help her. I saw how helpless she felt. It felt like I was watching myself through the screen, and in that moment, I felt less alone.

Then I watched Jesus take her in his arms. He cast out the demons that had tortured her mind, his touch and words healing her. My eyes lit up with hope. I felt so connected to her story, and I thought, *If he can heal her, why wouldn't he be able to heal me? Maybe I can have a second chance.*

After watching the episode, I went into my safe place, the shower. Angela, my other safe place, sat outside and talked to me.

I asked her, "Do you think Jesus will heal me, like he did with Mary Magdalene?"

"Oh, I know he will," she said. "All you have to do is ask him."

I took a deep breath, put my hands over my head, and prayed out loud: "Jesus, can you heal me like you did with Mary Magdalene?"

Later that night, I lay next to Angela and said, "Do you think I need medication?"

"No," she said. "Give it a month. Let's read the Word."

I knew the doctors who wanted to prescribe me medications for my anxiety were doing what they thought was best for my healing, but what I really needed was the truth—the Word of God.

As I read the Bible for the first time and learned the nature of who Jesus is, I felt like I could finally have rest in my soul. The crippling fear that had plagued me since I was a little girl finally began to slip away, and I was able to experience true peace. By reading the stories of Jesus healing people, I became resilient and began to develop a childlike faith. Light returned to my eyes, my mind began to be restored, the broken parts of me started to heal, and my anxiety subsided. I learned that my intrusive thoughts were not part of my identity. I learned how to fight and combat them with the truth—the Bible—and they lost their foothold in my life.[4]

Just like he'd done with Mary, Jesus found me in my darkest place and healed me. And like with Mary, my desperate longing to be close to Jesus and to serve him in any way I could became how I lived my life. Even though I once lived in fear, now I choose faith because he is with me. I rely on God and his Word as my rock and my comfort. Just like Mary, I know I would not have a life if not for him.

Dear Jesus,

I've struggled for so long to find healing, but now I surrender it all to you. You are the breath of life, the beginning and end of all things, the one capable of all things. Please heal me and bring my heart and mind into alignment with you. Help me to take captive every thought and make it obedient to you, to seek you above all and to surrender my life to you. Thank you for your mercies, which are new every morning, and for your love and healing. I love you.

In your name, amen.

Your turn: What have you learned about Jesus in this devotion, and how does this apply to your season in the wilderness?

_____

_____

_____

_____

_____

_____

_____

_____

_____

The Revealing Power of Fasting

Jesus said to them, "Because of your unbelief; for assuredly, I say to you, if you have faith as a mustard seed, you will say to this mountain, 'Move from here to there,' and it will move; and nothing will be impossible for you. However, this kind does not go out except by prayer and fasting."
—MATTHEW 17:20–21, NKJV

While they were worshiping the Lord and fasting, the Holy Spirit said, "Set apart for me Barnabas and Saul for the work to which I have called them." So after they had fasted and prayed, they placed their hands on them and sent them off.
—ACTS 13:2–3

In Acts 13, Barnabas, Simeon, and Saul were at the church in Antioch, fasting and worshipping, when the Holy Spirit called them as missionaries to spread the gospel throughout the world. The context surrounding this verse is not coincidental; God was revealing the importance of the spiritual practice of fasting and prayer.

There are a multitude of benefits to fasting, all backed by Scripture:

Fasting can bring clarity to the voice of God. (Acts 13:2)
Fasting can bring favor. (Esther 4:16)

Fasting can bring healing. (Psalm 35:13–14)

Fasting can prepare you for the call of God. (Matthew 4:1–4)

Fasting can bring protection. (Ezra 8:21)

Fasting can increase spiritual authority. (Matthew 17:19–21)

Fasting can develop a dependence on God. (Matthew 4:3–4)

From Angela

For me, fasting is hands down the most important and beneficial spiritual practice I have implemented into my life. I fast weekly as a way to truly humble myself before the Lord and live sacrificially for him. Fasting strengthens my faith and restores my spiritual life when I'm feeling depleted. It helps me practice physical discipline, since by giving up the satisfaction of eating, I am training myself to let the strength of God override any fleshly desires. This practice helps me be stronger in the face of temptation when it comes.

The first time I ever fasted was when we began *Girls Gone Bible*. The idea of starting a podcast was terrifying. It was all happening so fast, and Ari and I were truly the most amateur podcasters to ever exist. We had no idea what it was going to look like or how it would be structured. We just knew that God had radically saved our lives, and we wanted everyone to know. I was desperate for God to be in control and at the center of everything we did.

I went into that first fast with the hope that God would reveal to me what he wanted GGB to look like, and he showed up beautifully. He put on my heart a play-by-play of exactly how the show should be structured, how we should come up with topics, how we should *always* read the Bible (he was very specific with this part), how every episode topic would have a Bible story, and how we would testify to the truth of his Word through our own personal stories. (He truly is such a creative genius, and I love inviting him into anything I'm working on because he makes it all so much better.)

The way this fast brought such intentional clarity and direction had me absolutely hooked. I started fasting every week, desperate to hear from God.

My first multiday fast was all because of a guy. This wonderful, godly man and I had been talking for a very short time, but I was at the point in my life when I could no longer stay in a relationship if I didn't think it would end in marriage. I was just done. I didn't want another boyfriend just to experience another breakup. So I decided to go on a fast and ask God to confirm very clearly whether this guy was meant to be in my life or not.

Let me tell you: It's a big jump from a one-day fast to a two-day fast. I could almost tangibly feel the Spirit shifting and changing my heart and mind. The emptying and detox of my body became a physical manifestation of what was happening in me spiritually.

So I was surprised when God didn't immediately give me a clear answer. In fact, *during* my fast, I misunderstood my euphoria as heightened feelings for the guy. I was on such a spiritual high that I thought, *What if he is the one?* I had so much peace about it.

But a few days after the fast—listen, I can't make this up—I woke up and all the feelings were gone. The sudden switch almost gave me whiplash. I went from thinking I had total peace to feeling certain this wasn't the relationship for me. God had removed all romantic feelings for this guy, and I had a clear revelation that our relationship was meant to be a friendship. Even still, it took me a few days to process what had happened. I had to sit with God for a little while to reaffirm that this was what he had spoken. But eventually, I responded in obedience and ended the relationship.

This is how God will often speak to me. I'll pray, "Put on my heart,

Lord, how *you* want me to feel about this and give me eyes to see it the way *you* see it." And then he will answer me by simply shifting my heart to align with his will.

I look back on this experience with complete peace and know that it was the right decision. As usual, it left me in absolute awe and wonder at the way God moves. First, he elevated my faith and trust in his Word by proving to me that fasting really does work the way the Bible claims. Second, he gave me a sense of security through the spiritual tool of fasting. Ever since I first discovered it, it's become a consistent practice in my life but also something I lean on in times of emergency or upheaval. Whenever I have a 911 need for God's voice and direction, a need for spiritual restoration and revival, or even a need for protection when I feel under attack and in spiritual danger, I fast to keep my eyes focused on God.

I'm forever grateful for all the ways he helps us connect more deeply with him. He is so good, and his Word is complete truth. And since he's always speaking, we should make sure we're listening. Emptying ourselves physically is just one of the ways we can do so.

Dear Jesus,

Thank you for your Word. Thank you that it is absolute truth, from Genesis to Revelation. Help me to live by this truth. Forgive me for when I crave any created thing more than I hunger and thirst for you. I'm sorry for when the desire for the luxuries of life or even for my everyday necessities takes precedence over my desire and need for you.

Lord, help me implement fasting in my life as a spiritual practice. Teach me the biblical principles of fasting and open my eyes to its benefits. Show me how I can utilize it in whatever way I need to get closer to you. I offer myself as a living sacrifice—body, soul, and spirit—to you. Encourage me to no longer live by bread alone, but by every word that proceeds from your mouth.

When I fast, Lord, give me fresh vision and breakthroughs in whatever areas you see fit. Help me to experience healing and restoration. Empty me of anything that's not of you or from you. I give you permission to clean house during my fast—so that all I am left with is the Spirit of the living God flowing through me.

In your holy name, free me from all bondage, strongholds, and curses I'm not even aware of. Lord, use this fast to bring me to my knees in humility. May this sacrifice cost me, mirroring the way your sacrifice on the cross cost you. I receive all that you have for me in this fast.

I love you so much. Bring me closer to you.

In your powerful name I pray, amen.

Your turn: What have you learned about Jesus in this devotion, and how does this apply to your season in the wilderness?

_____

_____

_____

_____

_____

Day Twenty-Two

Do Everything in Love

Therefore, as God's chosen people, holy and dearly loved, clothe yourselves with compassion, kindness, humility, gentleness and patience.

—Colossians 3:12

The Lord looked with favor on Abel and his offering, but on Cain and his offering he did not look with favor. So Cain was very angry, and his face was downcast.

Then the Lord said to Cain, "Why are you angry? Why is your fast downcast? If you do what is right, will you not be accepted? But if you do not do what is right, sin is crouching at your door; it desires to have you, but you must rule over it."

—Genesis 4:4–7

It's so easy to get caught up in the game of comparison. *She's prettier and thinner than me. She's smarter than me. She's so secure and put together.* Whether it's your physical appearance, your career, your relationship status, or even your journey with God, it's so easy to look at the person next to you and feel bad about yourself. But God doesn't want you looking around and comparing yourself. He created every piece of you, and he loves you for you and for how unique you are. More than how you measure up to others, he cares about what's in your heart and how it's aligned with his.

When we compare ourselves and allow envy into our hearts, we're opening the door to sin and separation from God. Conversely, when we come to him and invite him into our lives, he remakes us and changes our hearts. The closer we get to God, the more we're able to walk like Jesus, who healed the sick and clothed himself in compassion, kindness, humility, gentleness, and patience. As we pattern our lives after his, we should strive to do the same.

From Arielle

In 2010, I competed in Miss Hawaiian Tropic USA—my first time doing anything like that. I was incredibly nervous, not knowing what to expect, but I thought, *Why not? If nothing else, I can meet some new friends.* When my plane touched down in Mississippi, I remember feeling so overwhelmed. And when I walked into the lobby to meet all the other participants, I thought, *Wow, these girls are so beautiful. They've been competing their whole life. I am not as tall or qualified as them. I don't stand a chance.*

The first day included a meet and greet, an event that ended up being my personal favorite because it involved talking to the other contestants. Two specific people that day—a mom and her daughter—caught my eye. The daughter had a chronic illness, but it was her dream to compete in pageants. I sat with the two of them and listened to their story, and the three of us took photos together. The daughter's story and their kindness made such an impression on me, and both women are still present in my life today.

The next day, we participated in a golf tournament. On the way to the event, someone else caught my eye. This time, it was the bus driver. He had lost his daughter a year prior, but God's light still shone through him, and somehow, he had such a positive outlook on life. We laughed and even shared some tears on the drive. His joyful spirit and God-centered perspective affected me so strongly that I am still inspired by him today.

Despite these incredible experiences, on the day of the pageant, I still couldn't help but think, *Why am I even here? I am not qualified for this.* Before I walked onstage, I closed my eyes. My vision filled with white, and I could sense arms wrapping around me, giving me an overwhelming feeling of love. I know now that it was the power of the Holy Spirit, showing me he was with me. At the time, all I knew was that I suddenly had complete peace and confidence.

As I walked out onto the stage, I felt so proud of myself for having the courage even to go out and be bold. They called third place and then second place, neither of which was me. I bowed my head, thinking, *I didn't win, and that's okay. I'm just happy I got to be a part of something so incredible and meet so many great people.*

And then I heard it.

"First place goes to Arielle Reitsma."

What?

I couldn't believe it. They literally had to re-film me winning because I looked up and said, "Are you sure it's me?" Typical Arielle! Haha!

After I won, the judges approached me. Imagine my surprise when I recognized the bus driver and the mother and daughter from the meet and greet. The organization had hired them as undercover observers to see who would actually give them the time of day. They wanted the pageant winner to be more than just a pretty face.

When I think back on the most monumental moments of my life, that one ranks as one of the highest. The whole experience taught me so much. Even though I spent so much time comparing myself and feeling unqualified, it was really about what was in my heart. When the judges chose me, it was because they saw me for who I was on the inside—which is far greater than anything else.

God is also concerned with our hearts and desires, and that internal purity is more important than external appearances. Jesus could have come down to earth as a king. After all, he is the Alpha and Omega, the King of kings. Yet he came down as a humble boy who grew up in poverty in a small town in Nazareth. A man who took care of the homeless, healed the sick, and embodied the greatest compassion and kindness of anyone in history. Whenever we get wrapped up in comparison or outward appearance, we should remember how Jesus lived his life. He wasn't worried about external things because those won't last. Instead, he showed by example how important it is to develop a rich interior life. As 1 Peter 3:4 says, "Rather, it should be that of your inner self, the unfading beauty of a gentle and quiet spirit, which is of great worth in God's sight."

I had spent so much of my life worrying about what I looked like, comparing myself to others, and trying to keep up with the latest trends. But although it's nice to feel good, the spiritual fruit of kindness, gentleness, and grace is what really matters. That's what honors the Lord. Peter called a gentle and quiet spirit a reflection of "incorruptible beauty" and added that such things are "very precious in the sight of God" (NKJV).

True beauty is inward. It is a matter of the heart. As Jesus said in his famous Sermon on the Mount, "Blessed are the pure in heart, for they shall see God" (Matthew 5:8).

Dear Jesus,

Thank you for all you have done for me. Help me become more like you, Jesus. Guide my heart, and grow me into the person you want me to be. Rather than letting me follow my own ways, please purify my heart and make me more like you. Let me always decrease while you increase in my life. I love you.

Anywhere that there could be deceit in my heart, please take it out and fill it with patience, joy, peace, and kindness. I love you, Jesus.

In your name, amen.

Your turn: What have you learned about Jesus in this devotion, and how does this apply to your season in the wilderness?

_____

_____

_____

_____

_____

_____

_____

_____

Tempted in the Wilderness

At once the Spirit sent him out into the wilderness, and he was in the wilderness forty days, being tempted by Satan. He was with the wild animals, and angels attended him.
—MARK 1:12–13

After his baptism, Jesus was led by the Holy Spirit into the wilderness, where he spent forty days and nights fasting. While there, he faced three specific temptations from Satan (Matthew 4:4, 7, 10):

1. Satan tempted Jesus to use his divine power to satisfy his hunger. Jesus responded by quoting Scripture, saying that man does not live by bread alone but by every word from God.

2. Satan took Jesus to the pinnacle of the temple in Jerusalem, told him to throw himself down to prove his divinity, and cited Scripture that said angels would protect him. Jesus countered with Scripture, saying that one should not test God.

3. Satan offered Jesus all the kingdoms of the world if he would only worship Satan. Jesus rejected this, citing Scripture for the third time to say that worship is meant for God alone.

Throughout these temptations, Jesus remained steadfast and used Scripture to reject Satan's attempts. Afterward, the angels came to minister to Jesus. This period in the wilderness served as a test of Jesus's obedience and commitment to his mission, demonstrating his reliance on God's Word and his rejection of worldly temptations.

From Angela

I think it's incredibly interesting that Jesus was tempted like this *after* his encounter with God during his baptism. In my own life, I've noticed how spiritual victories are often followed by temptation. It seems like every time I go deeper in my relationship with God, the enemy comes around with a temptation to rob me of my achievement.

In my early days of being saved, when I spent a year in isolation with Jesus, I was so in love with him and on fire for God. I had just gotten out of a two-year relationship and was on my own for the first time. I was sober, single, and fully devoted to God. That year was crucial for my faith since it was the first time God began a true sanctification process in my life and in my heart.

Sanctification, according to the Bible, means to be set apart and to be made holy. It is both an immediate and ongoing work of God's grace. There is *positional sanctification,* in which one is immediately set apart for God upon being saved (1 Corinthians 1:2). And then there is *lifelong sanctification,* which describes how the Holy Spirit helps one become holy and more like Christ over a lifetime (2 Corinthians 3:18).

That year right after being saved was the first time in my life when I was sensitive to sin, consciously aware of conviction, and considerate of God's opinion of me and my behavior. God was pruning me and sanctifying me so intensely—and I was loving it.

I had determined to take purity seriously and wait for a godly relationship. For the first time, I loved Jesus more than sin. I was so obsessed with him that it broke my heart to partake in anything that broke his. I removed myself from the world and cut myself off from people who were not aiding in my relationship with Jesus. I reached new heights in my faith and grew rapidly in Jesus.

Until suddenly I started experiencing bouts of extreme loneliness and a desire for partnership. I couldn't make sense of it since I had not only been content but also *thriving* in this isolation with Jesus. Driven by these old desires, I started dating, occasionally going out, and living more of an L.A. lifestyle, which was never who I was or what I enjoyed. It wasn't even that I was doing anything wrong, but I knew deep down that God had called me to be *set apart* for him. So even though this new lifestyle wasn't necessarily bad, it was still a major distraction.

I spent the next two years in a balancing act of being fully in the world and fully in love with and on fire for Jesus. I was the definition of "one foot in and one foot out." I loved Jesus so much, but I got caught up in the world. My heart was shallow soil, so even though the seed of Jesus fell, the roots were not deep and the plant died (Matthew 13:5–6).

Thankfully, God is gracious, merciful, and patient, and he understands. He was eventually able to get ahold of me again and bring me into an even more intense period of sanctification. This time, the seed was planted in good soil. The edifying Word of God took root in my heart and in my spirit while it was fertile soil, and it produced a crop that was thirty, sixty, and even a hundred times as much as had been planted (Matthew 13:8).

Nonetheless, I quickly learned that every time I did good for God, I was met with temptation. I even developed an understanding of why so many pastors and leaders of the church fall into temptation and end up in morally corrupt situations. The devil is after those who preach the Word of God. The bigger the impact, the stronger the attack.

When Ari and I started *Girls Gone Bible,* I had very clear instructions from God that he wanted me to remain single. He wanted me to be absolutely starved of any male attention or comfort from a man. It became one of the greatest challenges God would bring me through, since launching our podcast was the most vulnerable experience I'd ever had. I felt so deeply that I needed the stability and security I would find in a man, but God was adamant that it was time I found that in him and him alone. So I made a pact with God that I would be completely single.

During my new journey into ministry, I discovered something I called a holy hangover. Every time I filmed a heavy episode or did a big event, or after any situation where I poured myself out emotionally and spiritually, I would have a strong anointing hangover that left me feeling incredibly vulnerable, weak, and empty. That became the enemy's favorite moment to attack. Before I understood why this was happening, I would be tempted with my flesh's favorite vices and old, unhealthy thought patterns. Satan would get in my head, fill me with major doubt and insecurity, and make me question my entire existence in ministry. *Did God really say I'm worthy of carrying his name?*

When these holy hangovers first started happening, I often felt lonely and longed for the companionship I'd had in my previous relationships. But I couldn't understand why. Hadn't I just poured out my heart and soul for God and his people? I didn't really want a relationship, did I? I wanted to focus on Jesus. Why was I suddenly being filled with these desires that went against what God had spoken to me?

As I soon learned, though, knowledge is power and revelation is freedom. When I first read about Jesus being tempted in the wilderness after his baptism, I finally realized why these holy hangovers were happening. I realized it was no coincidence that these temptations were hitting me at my lowest, emptiest moments.

Armed with this revelation from God, I am now able to be on guard in moments when I know I will be emotionally and spiritually sensitive. Every spiritual victory of mine is for the glory of Christ, and there's no way I will let the guy who got kicked out of heaven rob that victory.

Dear Jesus,

I come before you with a humble heart, seeking your guidance and strength. I acknowledge that I am weak and prone to wander, but I trust in your power to sustain and protect me. I ask for your help in avoiding temptation and living a life that is set apart for you only. Lord, lead me not into temptation, but deliver me from the evil one. Give me discernment to recognize the snares of the enemy and the wisdom to turn away from them. Fill me with your Holy Spirit, that I may be empowered to resist the allure of sin and walk in your righteousness.

Lord Jesus, I dedicate my life to you. I want to be set apart for your glory and your purposes. Mold me and shape me into your likeness.

In your name I pray, amen.

Your turn: What have you learned about Jesus in this devotion, and how does this apply to your season in the wilderness?

_____

_____

_____

All Is Well

In the sixth month of Elizabeth's pregnancy, God sent the angel Gabriel to Nazareth, a town in Galilee, to a virgin pledged to be married to a man named Joseph, a descendant of David. The virgin's name was Mary. The angel went to her and said, "Greetings, you who are highly favored! The Lord is with you."

Mary was greatly troubled at his words and wondered what kind of greeting this might be. But the angel said to her, "Do not be afraid, Mary; you have found favor with God. You will conceive and give birth to a son, and you are to call him Jesus. He will be great and will be called the Son of the Most High. The Lord God will give him the throne of his father David, and he will reign over Jacob's descendants forever; his kingdom will never end."

"How will this be," Mary asked the angel, "since I am a virgin?"

The angel answered, "The Holy Spirit will come on you, and the power of the Most High will overshadow you. So the holy one to be born will be called the Son of God. Even Elizabeth your relative is going to have a child in her old age, and she who was said to be unable to conceive is in her sixth month. For no word from God will ever fail."

"I am the Lord's servant," Mary answered. "May your word to me be fulfilled." Then the angel left her.

—LUKE 1:26–38

I admire Mary so much as a woman of faith. Even in the face of something so unbelievable—downright impossible—Mary had so much faith in God. Rather than questioning or doubting, she surrendered herself to the Lord and his plans.

When things aren't going our way or we feel like the Lord isn't fulfilling our plans, we can often experience bitterness. But when we have a faith like Mary's and offer ourselves as a living sacrifice to God, we often discover that his plans are so much better than our own. Whether it's surrendering relationships, careers, or our plans and dreams for our future, there are things we will all have to give up in our pursuit of God. But God will never withhold anything from us that is *meant* for us. His plans are always greater, and they will lead us to a life of joy and abundance.

From Arielle

When I was twenty-seven, there came a time when I realized I hadn't gotten my period in almost a year. Thinking it might be stress related, I went to my ob-gyn, who diagnosed me with polycystic ovary syndrome (PCOS). PCOS can affect fertility due to irregular ovulation and hormonal imbalances. Since one of my greatest desires is to be a mom, receiving that kind of news was a shock to my heart. My ob-gyn told me that a change of diet could help get my menstrual cycle back, so I changed my diet. But still, no period.

When I was thirty-one, my long-term relationship ended. I was devastated. Along with my heart being crushed, I knew the healing process was not going to be an easy ride and that it was going to be a long road before I met anyone else. I also worried that I'd missed my window to be a mom. I can't even tell you how many people have said to me, "Time is running out! You'd better hurry up or you are going to miss your window." The constant pressure weighed so heavily on me. Not only was I grieving the worst heartbreak of my life, but I was also grieving the thought that I may never be able to have kids.

Around the same time, I began my faith journey with Jesus, and prayer and Bible reading were drastically saving my life. So I started talking to God about the way I was feeling. I cried out to him, "God, there's this area of my life that—honestly—cripples me to think about. Am I infertile? And God, anytime I start to remember what your Word says, I hear the voices of other people telling me that my time is running out."

As I meditated in prayer, I felt called to read from the gospel of Luke, which describes the birth of Jesus. In Luke 1:34, Mary asks the angel how she will become pregnant, since she is still a virgin. It's a fair question. But the angel replies that God, by his power, and through the Holy Spirit, will conceive in her a child, "For nothing will be impossible with God." Mary responds in faith and obedience, saying, "I am the servant of the Lord; let it be to me according to your word" (Luke 1:37–38, ESV).

As I meditated on this verse, I saw it as Mary saying something like this: "I hear God's plan. I want to go along with it. May God do whatever he wants with me to make his plans come to pass." As astonishing as what she had been told was, she did not keep questioning it.

So my prayer changed. I went from begging God to praising him and knowing I'd received a Word from him. I reminded myself that the Lord is with me; and if he is with me and for me, then I would make the decision that his word to me would be fulfilled.

Even when I am going through a trial or a test, God still sees me. He is still a good Father who will not withhold good things from me. And I can still depend on him, despite my circumstances.

Four months later, I got my cycle again and it stayed. It had not been consistent without birth control in years. Mustering up the courage despite my fear of what I would hear, I went to the doctor to get my eggs checked. After the ultrasound, I bowed my head in the waiting room and started talking to God, saying, "Whatever is in your will, may your word to me be fulfilled."

Finally, the doctor called me in. He sat me down and said, "This is extremely rare with your diagnosis, but you are in the one percent of women who have over fifty eggs."

I looked up with tears in my eyes and smiled.

Through my journey with fertility, I realized miracles do not happen just because you have a desire for something. Miracles happen because you have the faith for it. I asked God for a word, and "May your word be fulfilled" carried me through. Although I still do not have children, I do not let the opinions of others or the voice of the enemy trap me in disappointment. Instead, I remember the power of the name of Jesus and that all things happen on his timing and in his plans.

Maybe you're experiencing similar fertility fears or concerns, or perhaps you're facing another form of uncertainty in your life. Whatever you're dealing with, ask God to give you a scripture to stand on. Then when the doubts or questions surface—as they will—cling to the truth God has given you.

Dear Father,

I love you. I come before you, humbled and in need.

Lord, you know my struggles. I believe that you are a healer, and there is nothing too difficult for you. In the name of Jesus, I ask for a miracle of healing for myself. I ask for your healing touch to restore my body to its natural state of fertility. When I have fears, please give me peace. When uncertainties fill my mind, give me confidence. I ask in Jesus's name that you

give me a word to stand on through my season of waiting.
I submit my will to you right now. I offer my faith. May I be
your servant and may your word be fulfilled.

In Jesus's name I pray, amen.

Your turn: What have you learned about Jesus in this devotion,
and how does this apply to your season in the wilderness?

_____

_____

_____

_____

_____

_____

_____

_____

_____

_____

_____

_____

Overcoming Disordered Eating

The Lord said to Samuel, "Do not consider his appearance or his height, for I have rejected him. The Lord does not look at the things people look at. People look at the outward appearance, but the Lord looks at the heart."
—1 Samuel 16:7

I praise you because I am fearfully
and wonderfully made;
your works are wonderful,
I know that full well.
—Psalm 139:14

The first verse is part of the story where the prophet Sam-uel was sent by God to anoint the next king of Israel from among the sons of Jesse. Samuel initially assumed that Eliab, Jesse's eldest son, was God's chosen one based on his appearance. However, God corrected Samuel. The verse shows that human judgments are often superficial, focusing on physical attributes. However, God's assessment of people is based on their inner character and heart; his judgment goes deeper.

In the second verse, David was acknowledging God's intricate and masterful creation of human beings. He was praising God for the miraculous and intentional design of his body and self. This verse reflects gratitude, recognition of God's sovereignty, and the marvelous nature of his creations, encouraging believers to appreciate and respect their own and others' design.

From Angela

I often think of the younger version of myself. The one who began to be aware of her body way earlier than she should have. The one who was only seven years old, trying to starve herself so she could look skinny at the community pool. A child looking in the mirror, picking herself apart and pointing out everything she hated about herself. I have sat and had so many conversations with God, asking him why and when this started. Who made a comment they shouldn't have? Who judged my appearance? Who made me feel like I wasn't good enough? And how, God, has it stuck with me all these years later?

My complicated relationship with food began as early as I can remember. I'd started going on crash diets when I was in middle school, and in high school I would take medications that would ruin my appetite so I wouldn't eat. This was my normal and continued until my mid-twenties. I've battled a decade-long, silent war in my relationship to my body and to food.

OCD was the driving force in the acceleration of my disordered eating. The obsessive-compulsive part of my brain would cause me to have an all-or-nothing mentality. I would enter periods of extreme restriction and borderline starvation. Then, when I was left practically malnourished, I would find myself in an inevitable binge as my body begged for nutrients. Extreme abstinence from food is described as one of the "doctrines of demons" in 1 Timothy 4:1–3 (NKJV). This violent cycle and unhealthy relationship to food resulted in intense shame and self-loathing. Over the years, the disorder shape-shifted and took on many different forms. And I hated myself for it.

I developed safe foods and had a strict eating schedule. The second I was thrown off routine, sheer panic would take over. God forbid someone ask me to go out to lunch with them.

Constant thoughts of food and my body were wreaking havoc in my brain. Meanwhile, I tried to act like I was completely okay. But by this point, I just wished I would die.

I was fighting devils left and right, overcoming addiction and breaking free from all sorts of strongholds. But this area of my life went ignored and unattended to. I never once prayed against my unhealthy relationship with food and my body. It was simply something I accepted. I believed every single aspect of who God is—a God who heals, who delivers, who sets free . . . just not with this. I did not believe he could heal something that had been so deeply ingrained in me, something that was practically embedded in my DNA. It was part of me. And I believed I would have to live with it for the rest of my life.

But God began to press in and warn me that I needed to gain control over this area. I did not know where to begin. So I asked him. *Jesus, how do I recover from this?* And believe it or not, he told me I needed to fast and pray. I didn't understand how fasting would aid in my recovery as opposed to exacerbating it. But I listened to Lisa Bevere speak on how she fasted to recover from an eating disorder, and she said, "A diet will change the way you *look;* fasting will change the way you *live.*"[5]

With that in mind, I began fasting and praying consistently with the intention that God would heal my relationship with food. And because God is faithful and keeps his promises, it worked. I had thought I would struggle in this area for the rest of my life, suffering in complete surrender to it. But God began to heal me. I noticed my thought patterns with food becoming healthier, with significantly less anxiety around them. I no longer spent time worrying about what I would eat or whether I had eaten too much. I was able to see a more accurate view of myself when I looked in the mirror, and simply valued my body and the fact that it works every second of the day to keep me alive.

An eating disorder is evidence of a deeper turmoil within a person's heart. To overcome the eating disorder, it's crucial to address and heal the internal conflicts. Spiritual healing is an essential part of this process. Filling the void in your heart with God's love and truth is necessary for true recovery. Everyone has basic needs, such as trust, safety, control, esteem, intimacy, independence, and spirituality. Often, we're starving for our needs to be met.

Recovering from disordered eating and eating disorders requires relearning how to trust our bodies. This can be difficult because dieting and disordered behaviors often lead to distrust and disconnection from our bodies. As Christians, we can rebuild this trust through our faith in God the Father. We know that God created us, designed our bodies wonderfully, and that his design is good. Trusting God helps us trust our bodies too.

As I look back now, I can see how God has been so intimately involved in my recovery at every stage. I've realized that my disordered eating was never just about food, but also about deeper layers of hurt I accumulated throughout my life. But God in his mercy has helped reveal these, and with every hurt he uncovers, he faithfully heals.

Do I still deal with these issues at times and resort back to old thought patterns? Of course. It's an ongoing battle. But I'm not fighting in my own strength. I run to God in prayer every time something feels off, and he comes to my rescue without fail. We are co-laboring in my healing process from a lifelong disorder. Through him, I have gone from hopeless to hope-filled. I have seen that recovery is possible, even when it seems like it's not. The same is true for you. I promise you it is.

Dear Jesus,

I come before you with a mind clouded by the battle I face with my relationship with food and my body. Lord, I acknowledge my weakness and my need for your strength and healing. I ask for your divine intervention and the power of your love to set me free from this eating disorder and the unhealthy thoughts that plague me.

Jesus, you are the healer of all wounds, seen and unseen. I ask you to heal the deep-rooted pain and insecurities that fuel this disorder. Replace my distorted perceptions with your truth and help me to see myself as you see me—fearfully and wonderfully made. Give me the grace to treat my body with respect and care, to nourish it in a way that honors you. Grant me the wisdom to seek and accept the help I need, whether through counseling, support groups, or the loving encouragement of friends and family. Surround me with people who will uplift me and remind me of your love and promises.

In your holy and precious name I pray, amen.

Your turn: What have you learned about Jesus in this devotion, and how does this apply to your season in the wilderness?

The Darkness of Sorcery

This day I call the heavens and the earth as witnesses against you that I have set before you life and death, blessings and curses. Now choose life, so that you and your children may live.
—Deuteronomy 30:19

When you come into the land that the Lord your God is giving you, you shall not learn to follow the abominable practices of those nations. There shall not be found among you anyone who burns his son or his daughter as an offering, anyone who practices divination or tells fortunes or interprets omens, or a sorcerer or a charmer or a medium or a necromancer or one who inquires of the dead, for whoever does these things is an abomination to the Lord. And because of these abominations the Lord your God is driving them out before you.
—Deuteronomy 18:9–12, esv

A life without God leads to death. Today, people often look to the spiritual for comfort, but they're looking in all the wrong places. They're looking to healing crystals, manifestation, tarot cards, and psychics in their hunt for peace and reassurance. But the comfort they seek can only come from our relationship with and reliance on God. When we open the door to evil by participating in these unbiblical practices, we're choosing to follow false gods. And while some of these gods may seem harmless at first, we have to close the door and stop allowing false idols and practices to gain footholds in our lives.

From Arielle

Have you ever talked to your friends about something you're going through, then opened up your phone to find that exact thing you were venting about pop up on your social media's "For You" page?

That was my story. I would sit with my friends, bleeding out to them about the way I was feeling, and then I would go on social media and see a tarot reader giving me what I thought were the answers. I would think, *Is this a sign?* I started believing the answers the tarot readers offered, thinking it was the cure.

Growing up, I always went to tarot readers and mediums and never thought anything of it. So it stood to reason that when I faced challenges as an adult, I thought the same solutions would help me. I reverted to manifesting methods and seeking spiritual guidance from other people and things (false gods!), which only led me down a dark path of complete chaos and destruction. By relying on these false gods, I became bitter, prideful, destructive, and lustful. You might think practices like tarot reading or crystals are such a small thing, but in opening myself up to them, I landed in so many destructive situations.

Before I knew Jesus, I decided to take a trip to get away, which included a massage. The therapist I met on this trip told me she was a medium. She then started speaking things over me and telling me about my future. For the next three months, mediums would randomly approach me, speaking things over me to lure me in. It led me to question everything about my life. I started basing my days around what had been said to me, waiting on the edge of my seat for those things to come true.

One day, I walked out of my house and saw that a tree had fallen on my car, totaling it. I immediately knew something wasn't right, because the totaled car was only one in a string of disastrous things that had happened to me. Clearly, not only was my life getting worse, but *I* was getting worse. Feelings of shame were keeping me in bondage, and negative thoughts were overpowering my mind. At the time, I didn't understand that the enemy thrives on our vulnerability and weakness.

When I started learning from my pastor, Stephanie Ike Okafor, about the demonic realm, my eyes were opened. I could not believe I had been opening doors to this realm through tarot readers and mediums since I was a young girl. Pastor Ike says there are only two paths you can follow in life: The path of the world—the one the enemy wants you on—leads to death and destruction, but the path of following Jesus leads to truth and life. Life outside Christ is death. That's why he says he's setting a path before us to choose life or death. I learned this the hard way. But thankfully, I woke up and Jesus led me to the light.[6]

Psychics don't predict; they connect with demonic spirits that follow and study us from childhood up to adulthood. They tap into this communication with the demonic, and the weak and vulnerable fall for it in desperation. These demonic spirits then study us inside and out, figuring out everything we like and dislike and our greatest temptations.

When you agree to get readings, you are engaging in a demonic and dark practice. You are opening your very body as a home to demonic spirits, the same ones who know your weaknesses and will come after you with your greatest temptations. They will use the false idols of manifesting, astrology, tarot, crystals, and the like to pull you away from the truth of God. They have no power on their own. But when we choose sorcery, we are giving the enemy power and influence.

Pastor Stephanie put it this way: We have only one provider, and that is our Lord Jesus Christ. Our body is a vessel of the Holy Spirit, and the only spirit we should want is the Spirit of the Lord. When we recognize that God alone is our source and salvation, we no longer have to be controlled by other spiritual forces. When the joy, peace, hope, stability, strength, empowerment, and deliverance of God take root in our hearts, we can find spiritual safety in our Father. He is all we need.

When we don't know Jesus, we search for things to make us feel better. And often, that search leads us to false idols and other ideas that will harm us. But there is grace for that. In his mercy, God calls us back to himself and says, "Repent of your sins and turn to God, for the Kingdom of Heaven is near" (Matthew 4:17, NLT).

Dear Lord Jesus,

I acknowledge that I am a sinner, and I ask for your forgiveness. I believe you died for my sins and rose from the dead. I repent with my whole heart for my sins. I bind and rebuke any demonic spirit attached to my life. I declare that my body is a temple of the Holy Spirit and that no unclean spirit has permission to dwell in me. Thank you, Lord, that you have given me authority over all unclean spirits. I plead your blood over my mind, body, and spirit. Please cover every area of my life with your protection. Thank you, Lord, for your precious blood. Help me, protect me, and remove me from all evil, all demons, all bad spirits, and everything else that harms me.

In your name, amen.

Your turn: What have you learned about Jesus in this devotion, and how does this apply to your season in the wilderness?

_____

_____

_____

_____

_____

_____

_____

_____

_____

_____

_____

_____

Day Twenty-Seven

What's Done in the Dark

Blessed is the man who trusts in the LORD,
    whose trust is the LORD.
He is like a tree planted by water,
    that sends out its roots by the stream,
and does not fear when heat comes
    for it leaves remain green,
and is not anxious in the year of drought,
    for it does not cease to bear fruit.
—JEREMIAH 17:7–8, ESV

Trusting God when we can't see the outcome is hard. In the middle of desperate or dark situations, when God doesn't answer our call for rescue immediately, we worry he's abandoned us. That he doesn't care. Our nature is to try to control the situation, to find solutions on our own, impatiently working to protect ourselves. But these times are when God wants us to turn to him, to put our full faith and trust in him, to not be anxious or fearful, but to cling to him knowing that even in seasons of drought, he is fighting for us. When we fully surrender to God and trust in him, he protects us. While it's hard to find peace or rest when we know something is off, we have to trust that God is always faithful, even when we don't understand the big picture.

From Angela

I have always enjoyed my birthday. However, the year I turned twenty-six was different. It was sad, to say the least. Mainly because it marked the one and only time I was cheated on.

I had been dating someone new, and it was the most beautiful whirlwind romance. I loved him, and he loved me. I was convinced he was *the one*. Only a couple of months in, I told my mom, "I'm probably getting engaged soon."

But a few days before my birthday, I sensed a shift in the relationship. The intense love I had been experiencing had turned cold. There was a massive disconnect. A withdrawal. If you've ever been intensely loved and then had that person draw back, you know what I'm talking about. The shift caused me so much anxiety. So much confusion. So much pain. I knew something was wrong, but I just didn't know what.

Fortunately, my faithful Holy Spirit was moving and speaking and doing things in his perfectly divine timing.

I spent days in constant, desperate prayer, asking God to reveal to me what was going on behind the scenes. Had I done something wrong? Did he just not love me anymore? Was it all in my head? I was impatient and anxious, and I begged God to give me an answer, but it felt as though God had gone silent. Still, amid the soul-crushing anxiety, I faintly heard his voice encouraging me to be patient. The answers would come.

The night of my twenty-sixth birthday, my boyfriend was out of town for work, so I had a birthday dinner with my roommates. I told them my feelings and how the relationship had felt off. I was surprised when they all agreed that they believed someone else was in the picture. It was something I'd considered but hadn't really wanted to voice. That night, God spoke through my friends to confirm what he had already put on my heart. I excused myself to use the restroom. I unashamedly knelt on that bathroom floor and prayed: "Lord, I love you so much. And I know that you love me. Relieve me of this heartache. Expose what's happening here right now. I pray you position his heart to give me a complete and total confession. The truth will set me free. I receive your freedom from this situation. I believe it's already done. In Jesus's name I pray, amen."

I stepped outside, called my boyfriend, and asked him to be honest with me about why he was pulling away. And then, just like in the movies—*just like in the movies*—he confessed it all. He'd been texting a girl the week leading up to my birthday.

The sting of Judas. The kiss of betrayal.

Then he began to make excuses. She'd messaged him first . . . He just got caught up . . . He'd made a mistake . . . It was harmless. *Blah blah blah.* But I wasn't even as concerned with the betrayal as I was left in absolute awe and wonder at the way God had shown up for me when I needed him. My sweet God had used this horrible situation as a massive trust-building exercise between us. I thought God had abandoned me when I needed him so badly and was searching for answers. But God had orchestrated everything perfectly so that I would see his faithfulness through it.

This was a major lesson in patience and trust. God is God and I am not, and if he's not speaking yet, there's a reason for it. My job is to be truly still and wait on the Lord. Since that moment on the phone, I've never had trust issues when it comes to other people. Not because I trust *them,* but because I trust God. "God is light; in him there is no darkness at all" (1 John 1:5).

Waiting for God's voice amid chaos or pain can be excruciating, but we must learn to wait. To wait patiently. To wait expectantly. Because he's going to speak. He's going to move. He's going to come through. We just need to trust him.

Dear Jesus,

I love you so much. Thank you for being a God of truth. I'm so grateful that I am your beloved child and that you never leave me in the dark. Forgive me, Jesus, when I get impatient while waiting for a word from you. Strengthen my faith in these moments and deepen my trust.

I decree and declare that you would speak to me in every situation, and that I would hear you above all other voices. Give me eyes to see and ears to hear. Thank you for being fair, true, and just. Show me the truth, even if it hurts. I love you so much.

In your precious name I pray, amen.

Your turn: What have you learned about Jesus in this devotion, and how does this apply to your season in the wilderness?

Blessed Are Those Who Mourn

> Those who sow with tears
>   will reap with songs of joy.
> Those who go out weeping,
>   carrying seed to sow,
> will return with songs of joy,
>   carrying sheaves with them.
> —PSALM 126:5–6

Even as we have hope in the way this bigger story will end, it's appropriate to grieve when hard things happen to us or to someone we love. Sometimes we want to hide from our grief, and sometimes our sadness makes us feel stuck, which causes us to experience guilt. But God wants us to feel our hard emotions, not push them away. Even Jesus knows what it's like to suffer, hurt, and grieve, and he will meet us in our own sorrow. He doesn't just give us understanding; he also weeps with those who weep. Sometimes that mourning sneaks up on us when we think we're healed and made new. But we've learned that it's okay to go through grief again, if necessary. That's part of the journey with God, and he's right with us through it.

Grief, suffering, pain—these tough emotions make us more dependent on God, and we should see them as a blessing. Every tear brings us closer to him. There is no sadness, hurt, or loss he does not know personally. He can relate to all of it because he is the Man of Sorrows. Throughout his earthly life, Jesus experienced grief, pain, and loss. He wept at his friend's grave. He was misunderstood and falsely accused. He was spat upon by men and women he had created. He was betrayed by a so-called friend. (Maybe you know what that's like.) Yet none of this matches the indescribable pain he endured while hanging on the cross—in our place—becoming the only fully acceptable sin offering that we needed and God's justice required.

While he hung on the cross, in your place and mine, Jesus was separated from his Father for the first time in eternity. Jesus knows what you're going through; he understands the agony of loss. He not only says, "I love you," he also says, "I love you, and *I know.*"

From Arielle

Though I had been transformed, though Jesus saved me, I was still very much mourning the loss of a three-and-a-half-year relationship and grieving the death of dreams and plans of starting my future with someone I loved. It's been a very painful road. Although the renewal is beautiful, the transition was painful. As I walked in obedience to God, I was in a place of light. Everything I had prayed for all these years—peace, healing, joy, purpose—had come to fruition, and I thought, *This is a miracle.* Yet I still had an aching heart, which made me feel guilty because of all God had provided in my life. I wanted to soak into this new version of myself and all God's provisions, yet I felt like I was being robbed by the grief. My attitude seemed sort of selfish, even to me. After all, God had taken certain things away for my good. Yet here I was, still mourning it. I had transformed into the woman I had always dreamed of being, yet the shedding process was challenging, and I was going through a lot internally.

So often these past two years, it felt like I was taking two steps forward and then three steps back. A year passed since the relationship ended, yet I often felt I still had such sorrow in my heart. Maybe you've felt that way too—where some days the sun is shining and you're laughing with your friends, looking to God, thanking him for everything he's doing. And then other mornings you wake up with a heart full of grief, aching for someone to hold you and tell you, "This won't last forever," because at times it feels like it will.

One day, Ang noticed I was quiet and wasn't being myself. She knew something was wrong with me. "Are you okay?" she asked.

I tried to brush her off, telling her I was fine and everything was great. But she quietly said, "One of the most special things about you is the way you feel your feelings." She said that's why she believed God was able to do the work in my life the way he had, because I don't hold things back.

I immediately broke down in tears. I cried out to her, saying I was embarrassed that I was still hurting over this failed relationship. I felt I had a responsibility now, so how could I still be mourning over this situation? I needed to be strong, but lately I hadn't felt like I even knew who I was. Had I done something wrong to still feel like this? Was God mad at me? I didn't want to feel this way anymore. I was tired.

Do you know what happened after I let that out? I felt like I could breathe again.

I had been harboring those feelings because I had this perception that I had to be tough again, and strong, and I thought so much time had passed that I didn't have the right to still feel my feelings. Yet before we become strong, we must realize we are weak. Matthew 5:4—"Blessed are those who mourn"—is one of my favorite scriptures because it affirms that it's okay to actually feel my feelings. Doing so has given God the opportunity to really work inside my heart. When we hold things in, it makes us sick.

I remember bowing my head in prayer as God showed me my journey of pain and mourning. And then he showed me how he was right next to me through every single one of those moments, comforting me. In those pictures he shared, you know what I saw? How every tear brought me closer and closer to him. How it kept me dependent on him. That was his gift to me. Through my mourning, I found Jesus. I have gotten to experience and receive the most beautiful relationship with him.

Healing takes time. My best friend described it perfectly when she lost someone she loved. She said it was like the ocean. Some days it's steady and calm, while other days the waves are crashing into you, and you can't help but find yourself drowning in it all. Some days you find peace and serenity on a gentle surface, and other days the waves are so strong, they seem to hold you under. But then the ocean calms once more, and it gives you room to breathe again. The same goes for grief. Ultimately, as the saying goes, grief is love with no place to go.

My grief was as big and as deep as the ocean because that's how much love was shared, and to me there is nothing more beautiful yet painful than that. Feeling those feelings doesn't mean you're backpedaling. It doesn't make you weak. Being able to love as much as you did is a beautiful thing and a sign of strength.

Psalm 147:3 says, "He heals the brokenhearted and bandages their wounds" (NLT). God's heart is always for our healing. He wants us to be whole and restored. Yet, just like how the stitching of a physical wound is painful in the moment, we often undergo feelings of discomfort as we face our emotional pain and God binds up our wounds.

The beautiful thing is, God never leaves us in our pain. Anytime the Lord takes us through a healing process, he is always moving us to a place of greater wholeness and freedom.

Dear Father,

I love you. I lay my grief before you. I ask that you grant me the strength to endure this time of mourning, knowing you are with me every step of the way. I believe that you have a good reason for everything that happens and that you are always in control. And even when days of mourning come, it's because you are preparing me for better days. Although I know all of this, I can't help but feel sad and lost. I'm hurting, Lord. I come before you today for comfort. Bring healing to my wounded spirit and restore my hope. May your peace that surpasses all understanding guard my heart and my mind in Christ. I love you, Father.

In Jesus's name, amen.

Your turn: What have you learned about Jesus in this devotion, and how does this apply to your season in the wilderness?

The Cross, the Blood, and the Holy Spirit

For all have sinned and fall short of the glory of God, and all are justified freely by his grace through the redemption that came by Christ Jesus. God presented Christ as a sacrifice of atonement, through the shedding of his blood—to be received by faith. He did this to demonstrate his righteousness, because in his forbearance he had left the sins committed beforehand unpunished.
—Romans 3:23–25

Very truly I tell you, it is for your good that I am going away. Unless I go away, the Advocate will not come to you; but if I go, I will send him to you.
—John 16:7

Romans 3:23–25 is a key passage in understanding the Christian doctrine of salvation. Every person has sinned, meaning every person has acted against God's will and moral law. But God offers justification freely by his grace, meaning that we are declared righteous in God's sight. This is not earned by our effort but is a gift from God. Redemption refers to Jesus's sacrificial death, which paid the price for humanity's sins, freeing us from the penalty. God presented Jesus as a sacrifice of atonement. Jesus's death satisfied the demands of God's justice, making it possible for God to forgive sins without compromising his righteousness. The shedding of Jesus's blood is how atonement was and is made.

In John 16:7, Jesus was speaking to his disciples before his crucifixion, reassuring them that his departure was not a loss but a necessary step for the coming of the Holy Spirit. The Holy Spirit's presence among believers would not be possible unless Jesus first completed his earthly mission, including his sacrificial death and resurrection. The gift of the Holy Spirit ensures that his disciples are not left alone but are empowered and guided in their faith and mission.

From Angela

There are three biblical elements that hold great significance for me and for many other Christians, and understanding the importance of each one is a crucial part of strengthening our faith. They are the cross, Jesus's blood, and the Holy Spirit. Let's look at each one individually.

The Cross

The cross holds so much meaning and weight for me that I decided to get a cross tattooed on my body to have as a part of me forever. The cross represents Jesus's ultimate demonstration of love, sacrifice, redemption, salvation, reconciliation, grace, humility, and obedience. It also represents an instrument of death that was used in taking the life of our Savior. As the Gospels make clear, the crucifixion of Jesus was methodical and agonizing. First, he endured severe physical torment, being whipped and flogged. Roman soldiers mocked Jesus as "King of the Jews" by placing a crown of thorns on his head, pressing it down so the thorns pierced his flesh. Jesus was forced to carry his own cross to the place of execution, Golgotha, also known as Calvary. Considering the physical trauma from the flogging, this would have been extraordinarily difficult. As he walked, Jesus must have stumbled and struggled unimaginably under the weight of his cross. He was then nailed to it through his wrists and feet. The weight of Jesus's body pulling on his chest would have made it difficult to exhale. Jesus would need to push up on his feet to expand his chest and breathe, causing immense pain. Crucifixion was intentionally designed to prolong suffering, and Jesus experienced gradually increasing asphyxiation.

Crucifixion was not only physically torturous, but also the most shameful and degrading way to die. It was used for the worst criminals and slaves. Most statues and artwork portray Jesus with a covering over himself, but Roman crucifixion meant he actually would've been hung naked and exposed, enduring the most humiliating and extreme level of shame.

Replaying the reality of what Jesus did on the cross is the perfect remedy for apathy or numbness in my spiritual life. The word for "glory" in Hebrew stems from the root word for "weight," and it indicates that glory means to give something it's due weight—and the actuality of the cross should carry an exigent weight that sets our hearts ablaze for God every day of our lives.[7]

Jesus's Blood

Christians frequently talk about "the blood," saying things like, "I'm covered by the blood of Jesus." I went years not knowing the significance of it, thinking it was just some phrase Christians say. It took learning the theology behind the reason blood had to be shed for the forgiveness of our sins for me to understand and truly value the spiritual implications behind it. And seeing how "the blood" ties the Old and New Testaments together is fascinating.

Before Jesus, in the Old Testament, there was a system where animal sacrifices atoned for our sins. Hebrews 9:22 says, "In fact, the law requires that nearly everything be cleansed with blood, and without the shedding of blood there is no forgiveness." Depending on the type of sin, different animals would have been slaughtered as a sort of penance. But then Jesus came and stepped in to become the ultimate sacrificial Lamb of God. Unlike previous animal sacrifices that had to be repeated for each new sin, Jesus's once-and-for-all sacrifice was perfect and eternal. He died in our place and took the punishment we deserved. Likewise, before Jesus, we were unable to enter the presence of God. Instead, a high priest had to mediate between God and humans. But Jesus shed his blood and became our ultimate, eternal high priest. He reconciled us to God and granted us access to his presence. Ephesians 2:13 says, "But now in Christ Jesus you who once were far away have been brought near by the blood of Christ." We no longer need a middleman. We can come *boldly* to the throne of grace (Hebrews 4:16).

I call Jesus my best friend. He is so real and near that he is almost tangible. I see him, I feel him, I hear him, I know him. One day, I finally understood. It is only the shedding of his blood that makes this possible for me. Jesus couldn't be my best friend if he hadn't died for me. I would never know God the way I do if it weren't for the blood that Jesus shed. *Beautiful, beautiful Jesus, the Lamb of God who takes away the sins of the world. You are my heart and my life. You are closer than we think.*

The Holy Spirit

Jesus did not leave us as orphans. He left us with the precious gift of his Holy Spirit, my most prized possession in this life. The Holy Spirit is the third person of the Trinity (God, Jesus, and the Holy Spirit) and is often misunderstood, ignored, and even suppressed. He is not an impersonal force to be utilized, but a being that speaks, intercedes, teaches, and can be grieved. The Holy Spirit is my helper, confidant, and wise counselor. The one who encourages and empowers me. My purifier, who convicts me and leads me to repentance. My faithful intercessor, who prays for me when I cannot find the words. It is the work of the Holy Spirit that brings transformation to our lives and that reveals the divinity of Jesus to us. I love the Holy Spirit with all that I am.

The first time I encountered the Holy Spirit, I was at home listening to a sermon, minding my business, when I became completely overwhelmed with a sense that I wasn't alone anymore. A surge of power rushed through my body and filled my chest, and my hands began to tingle and get hot, as if they were on fire. This power pulled me down to my knees. The Spirit of God filled my room, and I began to weep and laugh uncontrollably. After that experience, I was obsessed with and in love with the Holy Spirit. I was so tender and sensitive to God's Spirit that I easily entered into the presence of God and experienced his glory. I discovered that this manifest presence of God causes us to fall to our knees in surrender and worship. But over time, I developed a fear that one day I wouldn't be able to access him. This made me approach him anxiously and hindered my ability to receive his touch. And then one day God reminded me of the scripture "Draw near to God, and he will draw near to you" (James 4:8, ESV). He gently spoke into my heart, *Either what I say is true, or it's not.* God keeps his promises, and if I draw near to him, he'll draw near to me. This instilled a confidence and assurance in me that every time I reach for him, he's going to show up, even if it's not always obvious or in the way I expect. Sometimes I feel like God is totally silent, but when I look back on those times, I see his fingerprints everywhere.

I implore you to develop a personal, intimate, loving relationship with the Holy Spirit. He wants to commune with you and walk in fellowship with you every moment of every day. He loves you and knows you and wants you to love him and know him back.

Dear God,

I come to you humbly, asking for the forgiveness of my sins. I confess that I have sinned against you and fallen short of your glory. I believe that Jesus Christ, your Son, died on the cross for my sins and that his precious blood was shed to cleanse me from all unrighteousness. I believe that he rose from the dead and is alive today, offering me eternal life.

I invite you into my heart to be my lord and savior. I surrender my life to you and ask you to guide me in your ways. Fill me with your Holy Spirit, that I may be empowered to live a life that is pleasing to you.

In Jesus's name I pray, amen.

Your turn: What have you learned about Jesus in this devotion, and how does this apply to your season in the wilderness?

_____

_____

_____

_____

_____

_____

_____

In Christ Alone My Hope Is Found

Glorify the LORD with me;
  let us exalt his name together.

I sought the LORD, and he answered me;
  he delivered me from all my fears.
Those who look to him are radiant;
  their faces are never covered with shame.
This poor man called, and the LORD heard him;
  he saved him out of all his troubles.
The angel of the LORD encamps around those
    who fear him,
  and he delivers them.

Taste and see that the LORD is good;
  blessed is the one who takes refuge in him.
                    —PSALM 34:3–8

The waiting season is something everyone is familiar with. It's the season of preparation before God does the next thing he's called us to do in life. These are the seasons when we have to fully surrender our trust to him, to believe that he is working for our good. Still, we tend to ask, *God, how long will this take? Do you even hear my prayers?* When we're in a place of fear or uncertainty, doubts creep in, but we have to hold fast to the promises of God. He will walk with us in our troubles and deliver us from them. He wants us to seek shelter in him, our good Father, and to depend on him and him alone. He is teaching and preparing us, always growing us as we seek him. Every challenging circumstance that comes our way is an opportunity to grow closer to him.

From Arielle

When I was younger, I imagined that as I entered my thirties, I would have a family, a beautiful marriage, and a home. Instead, I found myself at thirty with tears in my eyes and sadness in my heart, wondering how I got there.

I thought, *I should have my career in place by now. What am I going to do? My time is up. What else can I possibly do with my life? Why on earth am I in this place? Have I done something wrong to be set aside like this?*

Up until this point, I was always on the go. My priorities were my career and pouring all I had into the person I was with at the time. Now I was new in my faith and God had called me into a place of rest where I could be in total submission to him. I was to make him alone the priority in this season. In all honesty, sacrificing everything else was really hard at first. It wasn't pretty or sweet; instead, I was crying out to God in anger and in doubt: "God, why did you have to take that from me?" Thankfully, there is a serenity that comes with knowing that in our weakness, Christ is able to sympathize with us.

We tend to question and worry about why God removes certain things from our lives, not realizing those very things are what distract us from him. We fight to make things work, when God is saying, *Let it go! If you only knew what I have for you, you wouldn't be so resistant.*

I realized I couldn't rush or plead my way out of this season. I stopped fighting against my circumstances because I recognized that trying to control my season was clearly not working. I needed to let it go and accept that my ways are not his ways. He is a Father who is for me, not against me, so I put it all in his hands. And instead of asking questions about what I thought I wanted or needed, I asked God, "What are you trying to teach me in this season so I don't waste it?"

If we don't learn the lessons God is trying to teach us in our waiting season, he will keep taking us through them until we do learn. I know this because that is my story. Fighting against God's will and trying to do things my way only lengthened the time it took me to see what he actually had for me. Was it uncomfortable to go from having a career I enjoyed to working at a job I didn't love? Yes. Was it hard for me to be on my own for the first time? Extremely. But you know what that experience did? It humbled me. It drew me to him. It kept me dependent on him. It taught me the greatest lesson of all: He is all I need. God is so strategic with everything he does. I remember coming to a place of deep, godly sorrow and repentance and saying, "God, I am so sorry I turned my face from you my whole life. I didn't know better. Please forgive me." I felt an overwhelming love in return.

Everything started to make sense at that point. I realized God had been chasing me for so long, trying to get me to a place of intimacy with him, but my mind had been focused on everything else. I now entered a journey where it was solely me and God. I never thought it was possible to feel such safety, to be so completely at peace. Although I didn't have all the things I thought would make me feel fulfilled, I had him, and that was enough for me. My only responsibility was him. Instead of soaking in my trouble, I soaked my soul in his Word. I started meditating on his promises. Anytime unwanted thoughts filled my mind, I started declaring his promises out loud—that he will never leave me nor forsake me, that he is working all things together for my good, and that I do not need to fear because he will help me and strengthen me. As I started speaking these promises into my life each day, my strength was renewed. Even in hard moments, I stopped panicking and started trusting, because I knew he was with me, and that was enough. I realized God was concerned more about changing my character than answering my prayers. In my waiting, God was shaping and refining me. I slowly became more secure, bold, confident, and wise, not through a thing or a person, but through God.

I began ministering to the people around me, sharing with them the good news, which was more fulfilling to me than any job I had ever had before. I went from anxiously waiting to feeling satisfied.

After I had spent a year wholeheartedly devoting myself to God, he then trusted me with *Girls Gone Bible*. His answers and my waiting were never in vain. If he had given me everything I thought I wanted—the family and marriage, the career—I never would have found him the way I did. And finding him led me to find myself. The pain and the waiting changed me, and because of my trials, I was able to relate to and help others, like you. Without the waiting, I never would have found my best friend, Angela, who led me to something greater than I could ever have asked or hoped for—*Girls Gone Bible* and the family it created. Now that my wounds are scars, I'm able to share that God got me through my wilderness season, and he will get you through yours. He has a purpose and a plan. Don't be frustrated by what you don't know yet. God has a strategy, and it may be hidden until completion. The unfolding dynamics may not make sense till it's concluded.

My friend, God is preparing you for a blessing. And it's likely he has a bigger idea and a better plan than what you have in your head. But first he has to prepare you. What might look like the end is only the beginning. He already knows what he's going to do in the next year and in the next decade of your life. You simply need to trust him—relax in knowing that he's always on time.

Dear Jesus,

Thank you for this season of waiting and for what you're trying to teach me and grow in me. I want to spend this time with you. I ask, Lord, that you give me revelations as I read your Word. I ask that you help me to be patient and to seek you more fully in this time of surrender. Lord, I don't ever want to do anything my way or in my time. I ask that you shut any door that isn't meant for me. I trust you and believe that you're moving in my life and in my heart for my good. You are so faithful, and I praise your name.

I love you, Jesus. Amen.

Your turn: What have you learned about Jesus in this devotion, and how does this apply to your season in the wilderness?

_____

_____

_____

_____

_____

_____

_____

Day Thirty-One

Closer than a Sister

My command is this: Love each other as I have loved you. Greater
love has no one than this: to lay down one's life for one's friends.
—John 15:12–13

One who has unreliable friends soon comes to ruin,
but there is a friend who sticks closer than a brother.
—Proverbs 18:24

Jesus commands his disciples to love one another. This is
not a suggestion but a directive. Jesus set the standard for this love. He
is not asking for ordinary affection but for a deep, selfless, sacrificial
love, mirroring the love he has shown us.

In John 15, Jesus was teaching his disciples about the depth of true
love and the extent to which one should be willing to go for the sake of
others. This act of laying down one's life is presented as the greatest
expression of love, exemplified by Jesus himself.

It encourages individuals to be discerning in their friendships, recognizing that the company they keep can significantly influence their
well-being and life path. It also highlights the importance of nurturing
and valuing true friendships, which provide support, loyalty, and love,
often surpassing even familial bonds.

From Angela and Arielle

It was Ari's birthday, November 9, when I (Ang) saw her in the corner of the studio where we were doing a bridal shoot. We were strangers who should have simply crossed paths and never seen each other again, but God clearly had a bigger plan for this moment. Sweet Ari was weeping in her hands, trying to hide the fact that she was upset. I'll never forget the moment I felt a prompting of the Holy Spirit to go over and sit with her. Of course, normally if I saw someone crying in the corner of a room, I would go over to console them. But this wasn't an ordinary situation; there was weight to this moment.

I'm so big on obedience. Because God is so grand, we expect him to move in these massive and public ways—but so often, God works in obscurity. It's in my smallest and seemingly insignificant acts of obedience that I've seen God make waves and perform miracles. Obedience to that little voice nudging us and prompting us is so crucial in our walk with God. We must be sensitive to the voice and then move in obedience.

That day, it was as if the Holy Spirit gave me a glimpse into the future, because as I sat down next to Ari and took her hand, without thinking about what I was saying, I said, "I don't know who you are, but we're going to get through this together." And that's exactly what we would spend the foreseeable future doing—getting through it together.

We spent the next few years going to war for each other in prayer, covering each other and fighting for each other in the Spirit. Our friendship is so Christ-focused and Christ-centered that it has withstood many attacks. We are fully aware of the target that is on our friendship, and we are conscious of the devil's schemes to split up this divine partnership that only God himself could have orchestrated. We fast and pray together regularly with the intention of God protecting our relationship. Our communication leads to incredibly honest conversations daily. We fight like sisters and then get smoothies together ten minutes later. We are committed to maintaining the health of our friendship, and we love each other dearly, deeply, and so purely. From our beginning till now, there's never been a moment of competition, jealousy, or comparison—which is the work of the Spirit in us. We love each other so much that we want to see the other as better than ourselves. And we mean that. It is our priority to make sure the other is in the best position she can be. It is pure. It is truly the type of love that Jesus talks about when he says we must love one another enough to lay down our lives for each other.

Dear Jesus,

I come before you with the desire to find my best friend, a kindhearted spirit who sees me and accepts me the way you do. Who shares my joys and understands my struggles. Someone who can walk alongside me in the seasons of my life. Lord, as I seek my best friend, may your Spirit guide me in cultivating a heart that is open to receiving and reciprocating genuine connection. Teach me to be vulnerable, sharing not only my triumphs but also my challenges. Help me, Lord, to be a friend who reflects your love, grace, and kindness. I love you, Jesus.

In your name, amen.

Your turn: What have you learned about Jesus in this devotion, and how does this apply to your season in the wilderness?

Letters of Gratitude

As we came to the end of this book and finished our devotion on friendship, we were overwhelmed by how far we've come on our journey together to discover Jesus and share him with the world. Writing that devotion inspired us to write these letters, not just to you but also to each other. As you finish this devotional and reflect on all you've learned about Jesus, we encourage you to write your own letter of gratitude—whether it's to Jesus, to a good friend or family member who's been by your side through this time in the wilderness, or even to yourself—to remind you just how far you've come and to appreciate the gifts the Lord has placed in your life. Taking time to practice gratitude can give us a new perspective, and as you close this book, we encourage you to reflect on the things in your life that you're grateful for, even in difficult seasons.

I (Angela) wrote this letter for Ari, in light of what God is doing in our lives.

Dear Ari, my girl,

We have been through so much together—it's absolutely insane. The past few years of our friendship have been full of so much laughter and so many tears. Nobody has made me laugh harder, and nobody has comforted me better. You are my safe place and my voice of reason. You have a heart unlike any I've ever seen before. Your gift of encouragement has carried me through some of the darkest times in my life. Ministry is the greatest blessing, but it has also come with incredible challenges. That's just the truth. My joy has been attacked heavily and, sometimes, my sense of identity. I go to you, Ari, to remember who I am. I go to you to remind me of the joy that I know I encompass. You speak life into me and have an incredible gift of healing. You heal when you lay hands on people, and you heal them when you simply speak. I have the luxury of having your healing voice speak into my life daily. You are my favorite person in the world. I miss you when we're not together, and I describe myself as your "annoying little sister" because I ask you if you want to hang out every couple of hours. We resort back to being children when we are together, and we have the ability to speak a language other people don't understand. The way we laugh is something I've never experienced before.

Ar, I thank Jesus every day of my life for bringing you as my sister and my best friend. Nobody will ever know all that we've been through these past couple of years, especially after starting Girls Gone Bible. *I cannot emphasize this enough—I am so glad God gave me you to do this with. We have had so many shared life experiences and similar upbringings. Nobody could understand us the way we do. You are everything good in the world. I look at you, and I see a girl that Jesus looks at every single day and gleams with joy and pride because you are good, you are pure, you are special, and it's no coin-*

cidence that you're chosen. I'll never forget when you didn't feel qualified at the start of all this, and I'm sorry if I wasn't empathetic enough. But I honestly wasn't too concerned because I knew . . . I knew . . . the force that you are, the power that you have, and the gifts that you carry. And I knew the world needed to hear the gracious and powerful voice of Arielle Reitsma. I couldn't love you more if I tried. Thank you for being the greatest friend I've ever had. There is no one like you. Me and you for life, kid. Glory to God in the highest for bringing me you.

And I (Ari) share my letter to Angela.

Dear Ang,

I'll never forget doing a double take when you grabbed my hand in the corner that year on my birthday when I was in despair—when you quietly comforted and consoled me even though you didn't even know my name, telling me, "We'll get through this together." When I think back, I picture you as an angel coming down, rescuing me in your arms, and bringing me back to life when I was facing death. I was heartbroken over so many things, yet God provided me with something so much greater. And that is you—the biggest blessing God could have given me.

My sister, I believe that we are one, and I would lay my life down for you any day. I knew immediately you were special and called by God. You are a natural-born leader. You break chains of depression and addiction and heal with the power of your prayers. You make the enemy quiver when you speak with the authority of your words. Your love and devotion for Jesus is contagious and inspiring. The greatest blessing has been holding your hand and learning from you. You taught me everything I know about God. Every day you'd put aside whatever you were going through just to help me and disciple me. Your heart is selfless, and you'll go to war just to bring people out of the darkness and into the light. My biggest battle was my self-worth and mental health, and you taught me how to see myself when I couldn't, constantly speaking and breathing life into me day in and day out. You bring out the absolute best version of me because of how accepting you are. You have literally cured every lonely day and filled it with pure joy, peace, and laughter. When everyone walked away, you stayed, with God's glory in your eyes and a constant smile on your face.

You taught me how to be bold, to take authority, and to take the thoughts captive and make them obedient to Christ. You showed me what's important—sitting at the feet of Jesus. While everyone else has boyfriends and husbands, we have each other to get through every good, hard, and scary moment. I hope our future husbands will appreciate our need for connecting houses since we can't even go a week without each other. When you laugh so hard tears squeeze out of your eyes? We do that daily. What a gift. We have been through the depths of hell and back together, and I wouldn't want to do it with anyone else. Thank you for being the most loyal, dependable, non-judgmental, trustworthy friend. You are my world. It's me and you for life, kid.

And this is our letter to you, dear reader.

Dear friend,

Even though we've never met, we love and care about you so much, and we pray for you daily. We hope that your time spent in this devotional has made you feel less alone and has pointed you back to the feet of Jesus. The wilderness is lonely and scary, and oftentimes it feels like there's no light at the end of the tunnel. But there is a guaranteed light, and his name is Jesus. We are so grateful you would allow us to be on this journey with you, and we hope to continue pointing you to the source of life and hope. You are stronger than you think, and we will continue praying for you. And don't forget, you have Jesus, who intercedes for you himself, who prays to the Father on your behalf. The battle is won. The victory is yours. We love you. Jesus loves you more.

Love,

Angela and Ari

Your turn: Write a letter from your heart to someone who is important to you.

Acknowledgments

From Angela

To my Jesus: You saved my life and continue to save me every day. Someday, when I'm long gone and people think of me, I hope what they remember is "she really loved Jesus." Because I really do. Jesus, you have captivated my heart, and I will never be the same. I search for you incessantly, and I see you in everything. My heart beats for you, and my world revolves around you. Thank you for being my best friend. Thank you for the blood that you shed so I could experience you so closely. Thank you for choosing me and trusting me. This is the gospel—your taking someone who has no business carrying your name and choosing them anyway. You are a genius and a rebel and are so incredibly kind. As if you hadn't already done enough for me. I marvel at the reality of who you are. Most beautiful Jesus, I will love you till my very last breath, and I will follow you to the ends of the earth. I'm yours forever. Of this, I am certain.

To my family: Anyone who knows me knows you are my entire heart: my parents; my brothers, Neris and Xhulio; and Vilma; and my niece and nephews. I live for you. Thank you for loving me the way you do. You give me strength and confidence and an endless supply of love. God knows there is nothing we wouldn't do for each other.

To my mom, my beautiful Kristina: There aren't words to describe who you are to me. I wish every mother and daughter in the world could have what we have. Anytime I feel incapable or inadequate, my remedy is a phone call with you to remind me of who God made me to be. You have spoken life into me since I was born and have shaped me with your words. You are my heart and soul and pride and joy. There is no me without you. It's me and you forever.

To Socrates, the man who discipled me: You are the reason I know Jesus the way I do. You met me at the darkest and worst point of my life and always spoke to me as if I were already the woman God called me to be. You prayed for me and read Scripture to me and taught me to be a little warrior for Jesus. You changed the trajectory of my life, and I am forever grateful for the one who showed me who Jesus really is. In your famous words, "Hallelujah, thank you, Jesus."

From Ari

I am most thankful to my Lord Jesus. Jesus, I could never thank you enough for the love and strength you provide me daily. Thank you, too, for carrying me through the process of sharing my heart in writing for the first time. Anytime I doubt, you whisper, *My daughter, yes you can.* I am able to be at peace because I know I have a dad—you—who provides safety for me. You died to give us life, and I will never stop praising you for all you have done. Thank you for allowing me to be a servant in your kingdom, and for entrusting me to help the lives of this generation by sharing the good news and what it looks like to come out of the darkness and into your beautiful light.

Thank you to my mom, Roberta, and my dad, Michael. All the moments I doubted myself while writing, you guys kept nudging me, saying, "Yes, you can." Thank you, Mom and Dad, for all the love and support you provide for me.

To my baby sister, Gen: I'll forever remember staying up writing until 3 A.M. at your house and you quietly putting coffee by my bedside and providing a place for me to rest my head afterward. I love you, sister.

To Bobby and Noel (my second parents): Thank you for setting the foundation of how to believe in myself. You guys are and were my rock on the hard days of writing. Thank you for always being my sounding board of encouragement and strength.

To my best friends, my troops: Courtney, Ajia, Sam, Belen, Dee, Drea, Ang, Rachelle, Soph. What would I do without you girls? While I was writing this, I was still healing; you guys consistently spoke life to me through my late-night phone calls, reminding me of the journey you had walked with me as I wrote each of my stories. I love you guys.

From Both Angela and Ari

We both would like to thank our publishing agent, Esther. You believed in our stories, and it helped us believe in ourselves enough to write our very first book. Thank you, Esther, for standing by us through our journey.

Thank you to our collaborator, Katelyn. You were our rock while writing this book. Sharing our hearts in writing for the first time was the furthest thing from easy, but you held our hands during the whole journey, and we couldn't have done it without you. Thank you for being patient and believing in us so much.

We'd also like to thank the team at WaterBrook: Susan Tjaden, Leslie Calhoun, Laura Wright, Laura Barker, Campbell Wharton, Tina Constable, and everyone who helped bring this book together. We're so thankful you believed in us.

Notes

1. "Obsessive-Compulsive Disorder," National Institute of Mental Health, accessed October 30, 2024, www.nimh.nih.gov/health/topics/obsessive-compulsive-disorder-ocd.
2. Touré Roberts, "Winning the War Against Temptation," ONE | A Potter's House Church, July 31, 2023, YouTube, www.youtube.com/watch?v=vqLc9lrIab8.
3. Words in brackets are mine.
4. While I fully stand by my story of divine healing, if you are suffering from a medical or psychological illness, please also consult with a professional doctor or therapist.
5. Lisa Bevere, "A Fast Changes the Way You See [Fasting Explained] | Lesson 2 of Focus5 | Study with Lisa Bevere," Lisa Bevere, YouTube, www.youtube.com/watch?v=9Ylhx4Ew9_M.
6. Stephanie Ike, "Stephanie Ike & The Spirit Realm | Girls Gone Bible," Girls Gone Bible, April 26, 2024, YouTube, www.youtube.com/watch?v=TsMnPRJlGEM.
7. Avital Snow, The Weight of Glory and the Hebrew Word Kavod," Fellowship of Israel Related Ministries, July 24, 2022, https://firmisrael.org/learn/the-weight-of-glory-and-the-hebrew-word-kavod.

About the Authors

ANGELA HALILI was born in Tirana, Albania, to parents Edmond and Kristina Halili. Raised in Clearwater, Florida, with her two older brothers, Angela grew up with a close family relationship. In 2014, Angela moved to Los Angeles to attend the American Academy of Dramatic Arts, graduating in 2016 with her BA in acting, and continued to pursue a career in the field.

As Angela continued working in the industry, her struggle with alcohol and her mental health eventually led her to church and to her Savior, Jesus. As Jesus transformed Angela's life, his divine intervention connected her to Arielle Reitsma. Becoming fast friends, the two bonded deeply as they explored their newfound faith together, eventually starting their podcast, *Girls Gone Bible*, to show how God was moving in their lives and to point those searching for God to the feet of Jesus. Through their podcast, Angela loves sharing the joy and healing power of Jesus with others and working to change the current culture. Angela is an evangelist, and her greatest passion is watching people get saved and come home to God. She is dedicated to sharing God's Word, and her goal is to be remembered by how much she loved Jesus and his people.

. . .

ARIELLE REITSMA grew up in the small coastal town of Weymouth, Massachusetts, as the middle child of three. At the age of seventeen, Ari packed up and moved to the West Coast—all on her own—to build a better life for herself and to pursue her dreams as an actress and model in Hollywood. Having always carried a deep desire to help others, Ari found a renewed mind by renewing her faith in Jesus Christ and was eager to share this new peace with others. With new purpose, Arielle became inspired to lead others in transforming their lives by sharing how Jesus transformed hers. By divine intervention, that same Jesus partnered her with her best friend, Angela Halili, sending them off in a brand-new direction. Together with Angela, Ari co-founded the renowned podcast *Girls Gone Bible* as a ministry for mental health, community, and spreading joy. The weekly broadcast she endearingly describes as "Jesus for Degenerates" has only grown over time. As they've expanded beyond Hollywood's reach, Ari and Angela have taken their podcast to the stage with a national tour, spreading the message of Jesus across the country and, eventually, overseas. Speaking on different platforms and at engagements and conferences, Ari continues to champion the gospel of Christ using her personal message of mental health management, confidence, and heartbreak. Always looking for more ways to serve God, Arielle has an ever-growing heart for helping children at local ministries and churches and hopes someday to build homes for those in need. In her own words, Arielle is dedicated in her God-given mission of "sharing the gospel by sharing my heart."

About the Type

This book was set in Legacy, a typeface family designed by Ronald Arnholm (b. 1939) and issued in digital form by ITC in 1992. Both its serifed and unserifed versions are based on an original type created by the French punch cutter Nicholas Jenson in the late fifteenth century. While Legacy tends to differ from Jenson's original in its proportions, it maintains much of the latter's characteristic modulations in stroke.